Humanism

ALSO AVAILABLE FROM BLOOMSBURY

Humanism and Embodiment, Susan E. Babbit

Religion in Hip Hop, edited by Monica Miller, Anthony B. Pinn and Bernard "Bun B" Freeman

Secularization and Its Discontents, Rob Warner

Christianity and the University Experience, Matthew Guest, Kristin Aune, Sonya Sharma and Rob Warner

Humanism

Essays on race, religion, and cultural production

ANTHONY B. PINN

Bloomsbury Academic
An imprint of Bloomsbury Publishing Plc

B L O O M S B U R Y
LONDON • NEW DELHI • NEW YORK • SYDNEY

Bloomsbury Academic
An imprint of Bloomsbury Publishing Plc

50 Bedford Square
London
WC1B 3DP
UK

1385 Broadway
New York
NY 10018
USA

www.bloomsbury.com

BLOOMSBURY and the Diana logo are trademarks of Bloomsbury Publishing Plc

First published 2015

© Anthony B. Pinn, 2015

Anthony B. Pinn has asserted his right under the Copyright, Designs and Patents Act, 1988, to be identified as Author of this work.

All rights reserved. No part of this publication may be reproduced or transmitted in any form or by any means, electronic or mechanical, including photocopying, recording, or any information storage or retrieval system, without prior permission in writing from the publishers.

No responsibility for loss caused to any individual or organization acting on or refraining from action as a result of the material in this publication can be accepted by Bloomsbury or the author.

British Library Cataloguing-in-Publication Data
A catalogue record for this book is available from the British Library.

ISBN: HB: 978-1-4725-8141-9
PB: 978-1-4725-8142-6
ePDF: 978-1-4725-8143-3
ePub: 978-1-4725-8144-0

Library of Congress Cataloging-in-Publication Data
A catalog record for this book is available from the Library of Congress.

Typeset by Deanta Global Publishing Services, Chennai, India

Dedicated to

Lillian Floyd-Thomas
Linus Guillory, III
Izara Ide Knight
Benjamin Valentin
Gabriel Valentin

Contents

Acknowledgments viii

Introduction: Sisyphus, humanism, and
 the challenge of three 1

SECTION ONE   Race 11

1 Racing humanism: Two examples for context 13
2 African Americans living li(f)e 23
3 The ongoing challenge of race 29
4 Does race have a religion? On the "Faith" of Du Bois 40

SECTION TWO   Religion 55

5 Nimrod is a hero . . . and God is a problem 57
6 Humanism and the rethinking of a King's King 68
7 Putting Jesus in his place 76
8 Gathering the godless: Intentional "Communities" and ritualizing ordinary life 93

SECTION THREE   Cultural production 113

9 Learning to be cool, or making due with what we do 115
10 End of the "End": Humanism, hip-hop, and death 127
11 Speaking in public: The problem of theistic language for collective life 136

Epilogue: Sisyphus's happiness 147

Notes 153
Bibliography 168
Index 173

Acknowledgments

This book has developed over the course of years, and it follows my shifting thoughts on humanism. Many people and organizations provided opportunity to think through the issues that shape this volume, and I thank them all. In addition, my students and colleagues continue to provide important challenges and insights that sharpen my ideas and arguments. I must thank Cleve Tinsley, one of my graduate students, for his work on the bibliography of this volume. I owe a debt of gratitude to my editor, Lalle Pursglove, for her encouragements and advice over coffee in London and through too many emails to count. Thank you! Finally, I write these words mindful of the growing number of humanists and atheists, and I honor what it means for them to claim such a marginal (but important position). I am grateful for their company on this journey, and I hope the thoughts contained in this volume do justice to the long tradition of which they are a part.

Introduction: Sisyphus, humanism, and the challenge of three

In his essay on Sisyphus, Albert Camus ends with these haunting words: "one must imagine Sisyphus happy."

Written in 1955, two years before Camus received the Nobel Prize for Literature, *The Myth of Sisyphus and Other Essays*, in which one finds that essay on Sisyphus, explores the human's encounter with the world as absurd. More to the point, it wrestles with the appropriate response to absurdity. Is it suicide? That is to say, is the killing of oneself in light of the human condition, the existential angst and ontological trauma we face, a proper resolution to our dilemma? Camus answers, "no." Even in the absence of God, suicide is not the proper response to the challenges of our existence. But, is there something—despite the absurdity involved—that humans may grab hold of and anchor themselves to, as that which constitutes the reason life should continue? Camus answers, "yes." While some wallow in nihilistic thought and tendencies, Camus—without God—pushes for something more. He sees in the struggle(s) against nihilism, against injustice, and so on, the stuff of a worthy existence—the purpose of a life without certainties.

"Sisyphus . . . happy." I am continuously drawn to the sentence, and the request we see Sisyphus's punishment as not crushing him. As the story goes, Sisyphus is punished by the gods for a crime—a failure to remain in the land of the dead:

> It is said also that Sisyphus, being near to death, rashly wanted to test his wife's love. He ordered her to cast his unburied body in the middle of the public square. Sisyphus woke up in the underworld. And there, annoyed by an obedience so contrary to human love, he obtained from Pluto permission

to return to earth in order to chastise his wife. But when he had seen again the face of this world, enjoyed water and sun, warm stones and the sea, he no longer wanted to go back to the infernal darkness.[1]

Unwilling to heed the demands of the gods, he had to be forced back where he was punished by having to roll a rock up a hill. And upon reaching the top, the rock would roll back down, and he would start the task again in a perpetual loop. It was assumed this would be a deep and torturous process—something akin to the absurdity of life faced by humans. Sisyphus pushes his rock, but gains no meaning, no progress, in that the rock rolls down each time and he continues the task without conclusion—just as humans encounter and move through a world that does not respond to us, that offers us no lasting meaning.

My aim here is not to romanticize the individual's quest for "something." Instead, I want to hold in productive tension the individual and the collective so as to value both the private struggle and the need for community. Alain de Botton asks, "Could it be possible to reclaim a sense of community without having to base it on religious foundations?"[2] and I—with a slight alteration from "religious foundations" to theistic foundations—say yes. I view Sisyphus as dynamic, that is to say, as representing both our situation as individuals and the situation for communities. Again, the answer to imagining Sisyphus happy is lodged in ethics—in the manner in which we work to advance the potentialities of life for ourselves and for others. The grand individual, shoulder down, pushing for his or herself is a bad idea—a miserable approach we do well to reject. Instead, humanism does better through a turn to the individual within the context of community. Pushing that rock need not be a lonely enterprise.

Humanism on the ground

Sisyphus, from my perspective, speaks to a mode of humanism—that stance toward life that rejects the demands of gods and smirks at metaphysics meant to push humans beyond their flesh in the world. This humanism, over time, has been named in a variety of ways—for example, secular humanism, religious humanism, African American humanism, and humanism (without a qualifier but typically betraying European or white normativity). These qualifiers are meant to provide a particular cartography of engagement, or geography of community regarding those who embrace humanism to do a particular type of work. And while there are sociocultural, political, and economic differences represented by these various namings of humanism, I believe there is still a shared set of markers of meaning running across the particulars. I have, for a good number of years now, argued for the following as basic humanist principles, a sort of rudimentary framing of a humanist posture toward the world:

1. Recognition that humanity is fully and solely accountable and responsible for the human condition and the correction of humanity's plight. In this regard, humans constitute only a small dimension of life and must act in ways that recognize the web of existence as opposed to a simple assertion of humanity that ignores our interconnectedness.

2. General suspicion toward or rejection of supernatural explanations and claims, combined with an understanding of humanity as an evolving part of the natural environment as opposed to being a created being. This can involve disbelief in god(s).

3. An appreciation for cultural production and a perception of traditional forms of religiosity as having cultural importance as opposed to any type of "cosmic" authority.

4. A commitment to individual and societal transformation.

5. A controlled optimism that recognizes both human potential and human destructive activities.[3]

This is a *humanist* approach to living in that it recognizes no transcendent forces, and seeks to understand life only within the context of empirical, historical materials. It is *secular* in that it seeks to confine to private life the workings of theistic sensibilities and inclinations and in this way it guides public life based on governmental structures beholden to no particular religious tradition but committed to safe guarding private adherence to any tradition. The potentiality of democratic principles as the modus operandi of public/collective life—without theistic doctrine/creed clouding thought and shaping conversation—is the guiding desire. It is a *movement* because there is an orchestrated and systematic effort to work across lines based on a shared motivation and goal. Various organizations—such as the American Humanist Association and Atheist Alliance—have significant differences but collaborate based on a common concern to detangle public life from theistic experience.

This way of thinking and doing—humanism—has a long history that points in a variety of geographic directions. It is mapped in expansive ways that push well beyond the intellectual and cultural boundaries of Europe. Camus, the North African, is but one example and a recent one at that; but, humanist principles such as some of those I have outlined above extend into the "Middle East," Africa, and so on—going back many centuries. Humanism's reach and import have garnered it a good number of adherents as well as detractors—both speaking and writing their perspectives and opinions.

Some of what remains relatively muddy despite all of this attention involves fundamental ideas. For example, *how does humanism actually function in the world?* Much of what humanists and humanist organizations promote offers a soft response to such questions that highlights efforts to detangle church and state, and in this way push theism out of the public arena by preventing it from informing and influencing public policy, public principles and structures of relationship, and so on.

What concerns humanists?

This other question frequently asked seems answered through the strong and vocal attention given to science and science education, as humanists work to keep religious doctrine (e.g., creationism) out of public education. How does humanism interact with the cultural worlds that contain something of human strivings, desires, hopes, dreams, and fears? Some respond with attention to high culture (e.g., the "masters" of music and literature) and to the strivings of science to understand the human animal and what it does.

Is humanism just a type of religion, one meant to replace more evangelical modes of meaning make?

Many humanists I have encountered—outside Ethical Culture and the Unitarian Universalist Association (UUA)—cringe when hearing this question. They are eager to separate themselves and their "movement" from anything that even hints at the religious. For them the religious/religion is the structural trappings of small minds that imagine ghosts, gods, and other elements of superstition; and then these minds seek to make their ruminations the basis of public policy and practices. And then there is the issue of diversity—a stumbling block for humanist organizations and the general movement. The few "spots" of color within a given audience, the occasional "person of color" invited to speak (typically) on issues of race, only make graphic what is well known: the humanist movement is rather monochromatic. When race is discussed it is often (but not always) discussed in a way that lends itself to Eurocentric assumptions, anecdotal pronouncements turned into "objective" fact, and a defensive posture. At times this posture and the conversation it supports give the impression one should assume embrace of humanism is a prophylactic against racism and other modes of injustice.

Of course, what I have noted above does not capture all there is to say about humanism and its relationship to race, religion, and cultural production. Humanist communities are complex, and perspectives range; yet, there is at least a subtle truth in what I suggest in terms of a discomfort with deep probing within the movement of these particular issues. On these topics, well-spoken humanists often fail to find adequate words.

This triadic structuring of conversation, or the challenge of three—race, religion, and cultural production—is significant for humanists and the humanist movement precisely because they have perplexed "us." (I do not want it assumed that I see myself existing outside the context of this crisis.) This may be especially the case in the United States, where the outcome of humanist struggle for numerical growth and public space is still undetermined. It is to this need for clarity in the US humanist context that motivates this book. These chapters—in the sense of a chapter as a thought experiment, a proposition explicated with a bit of fluidity and intellectual flexibility—provide ways to think about each of these three linchpins of humanism in the world. I am convinced they buttress the structure(s) of humanism, and therefore demand ongoing attention, if humanism is to be understood within the larger society and if it is to meet the needs of a growing population of "seekers."

What I offer here involves my critical reflection on these three challenges written over the course of a good number of years—and I present these chapters mindful of the prodding of Camus: imagine . . . happiness by embracing the messy tasks associated with complex living in this world. The absurdity of our encounters with the world and the flimsy nature of our struggle to counteract this absurdity mark life. From my perspective, these three challenges constitute something of the "rock" humanists struggle to push.

Why another book on humanism?

Recent studies point to a change in the demographics of the United States, marked most profoundly by the religiously unaffiliated, or what we have come to call the "Nones." Spread across generations, this group encompasses a wide range of philosophical and ideological perspectives—some in line with forms of theism, others are more solidly atheistic, and all sorts of combinations in between. Scholars and the general public have a fascination with this group, and this general interest has sparked increased attention to the nature and meaning of humanism.

Numerous books addressing dimensions of humanist thought and/or practices are published each year. However, much of this work involves an effort to explain the superiority of humanism through the lens of the "natural" sciences and the social sciences (e.g., neuroscience). Less attention is given to description and analysis of the cultural worlds to which humanists respond and through which humanism develops. As a result, the general understanding of humanism is warped, tied to the "what" of life but with little attention to "how" life is arranged—socialized, ritualized—and framed in light of sociocultural markers such as race and religion. Furthermore, rarely is much substantive attention given to what the humanities (e.g., religious studies and cultural studies) offer regarding the relationship between humanism and these particular markers of our cultural worlds—race, religion, and popular culture. In short, the value of a humanities perspective on the nature and meaning of humanism is downplayed.

This collection of chapters provides an important corrective to this situation by offering humanities-based analysis and description of humanism in relationship to these cultural markers—race, religion, and popular culture. In so doing it holds in creative tension two areas of consideration: (1) what humanism says about or to these cultural markers, and (2) how these sociocultural constructs inform humanism. Furthermore, readers will note the manner in which issues of race, religion, and cultural production overlap in these chapters. Each of these three challenges informs and influences the others in such a way that the codes of race inform the cultural world of religion; and, the cultural world of religion effects that of race—and both are expressed through cultural production. And mindful of this, the chapters do not isolate each of these three but instead the chapters work to demonstrate their synergistic relationship. To do otherwise, I suggest, would be to present an artificial depiction, as if they are discrete categories without entanglements. Working in this manner also urges recognition that groups can learn something about themselves by viewing issues from the perspective of others. For example, white Americans should not believe materials only concern them when these materials highlight them and speak from their particular racial context. White Americans learn something about themselves by viewing issues of race, religion, and cultural production, for instance, from the perspective of African Americans. There is something *very* "American" about African American postures toward the world.

Little has been written that brings into play all three areas discussed in this volume—race, religion, and cultural production. On race, works by Williams Jones, Norm Allen, Michael Lackey, Sikivu Hutchinson, and Anthony Pinn constitute the bulk of available material.[4] And while the various books they have produced are important, much of their work entails an apologetic approach. This book offers a corrective in that it seeks to push beyond apologetics to robust description, contextualization, and application. Furthermore, much of the work—with a few notable exceptions—related to religion simply attacks theism while providing little analysis of religion and humanism's relationship to it.[5] *Humanism* extends the conversation by exploring both the differences between theism and humanism as well as points of convergence to the degree each concerns the formation of life meaning. In addition, this book is one of few written by someone with expertise in the study of humanism, race, and religion. Finally, while some attention has been given to humanism and culture it typically involves consideration of "high" culture (e.g., Nauert 2006; Witt 2012), and such work assumes a modernist and Enlightenment orientation. Less concern is given to popular culture, particularly elements of popular culture that challenge certain modern and Enlightenment notions (e.g., human progress).

Framing the chapters

In short, to my knowledge, this book is the first to bring these three important topics—race, religion, and cultural production—together in an explicit manner. It does this by offering previously published articles, plus two new chapters. Because these pieces were published for the most part in obscure locations, they have not received a wide readership and, as a result, they still have a great deal of "life" left. Furthermore, because the majority of these pieces were written for a general reader, they provide much needed information in a way that cuts across an academic and popular audience. In addition to these pieces, this introduction and conclusion provide the rationale for the volume as well as the intellectual links that give the book "flow." There is some overlap between the chapters, but I do not see this as a problem; rather, I believe it provides continuity and demonstrates the manner in which my thinking on these issues has grown over time.

The first section, on race, is composed of four pieces. All four are meant to interrogate the manner in which the racialization of human experience is played out within the context of humanist thought and action. While the first chapter provides a typology of humanism and toys with the idea of "shadow" humanism as undergirding much of the liberal religion found within African American communities, the remaining chapters in that section concern themselves with nontheistic humanism. In the second chapter, attention is given to the manner in which this godless approach to living becomes a means by which African Americans address the dehumanization embedded in social life by safeguarding the integrity of their being and this being within the context of a larger web of life. It also points to ways in which the larger humanist movement might go about embracing the dynamics of African American humanism and in this way revitalize itself. Assuming that most humanists are at least rhetorically committed to antiracism work, the third chapter uses the murder of Trayvon Martin as a case study for thinking through what it would mean for humanists to work actively against racial violence. The final chapter gives attention to recent scholarship on W. E. B. Du Bois to raise questions concerning the perceived importance of personal theistic conviction for those who speak about religion. That is to say, this chapter uses the case study of Du Bois to raise questions concerning what is at stake in the labeling theistic of particularly significant figures.

The second section on religion includes four pieces. The first explores and celebrates the humanist impulse underlying the story of Nimrod. I have argued for some time that Prometheus and Sisyphus (despite how much I appreciate Camus's take on the myth) are not the only heroes of humanism deserving of attention. In this chapter I reread the biblical story of Nimrod for what it says about: (1) death dealing nature of claims to transcendent authority; and (2) the importance of human creativity, determination, and collective commitment. The next chapter provides a rethinking of Martin L. King, Jr's theology and explores how a humanist hermeneutic might provide a more productive take on his thinking, and the larger issue of moral evil in the world in part by "humanizing" transcendent authority. One objective behind this chapter is to encourage humanists to take theology seriously as a methodological tool and to encourage humanists to critique theistic theological formulation without condemnation, and in this way preserve even the slim possibility of solidarity with liberal theists on issues of shared concern. Following this attention to King is a chapter that seeks to evaluate Christology (or the study of Jesus the Christ) from a humanist perspective. Because so much of Christian thought and ethics involves an extended Christology, I believe it is important humanist understand and be equipped to interrogate what is believed about Jesus the Christ. Tied to this attention to Jesus is a concern with the manner in which religious thought often reenforces bad notions of "blackness" and "whiteness," and in the process relies on scripture's rather poor understanding of the nature and meaning of humanity. The section ends with a chapter that addresses Sunday Assembly and humanist communities. In recent years, there has been a renewed turn to structures by means of which humanists might address the need for community and all this need entails. This chapter raises questions concerning the problematic of these humanist organizations basing their ritual model (e.g., order of service) on theistic churches. It concludes with ways humanists might forge and celebrate community without the stumbling block posed by modeling theistic organizations.

The final section on cultural production highlights a mode of expression rarely discussed within humanist circles—hip-hop. What do humanists want to achieve? What are the benchmarks for success? I argue humanism must entail more than the destruction of gods and the structures supported by such markers of transcendence. Furthermore, the first chapter suggests humanists must be true to their call for healthier life options through modes of engagement that are distinctive and organically humanistic in orientation. For help with this, I present ways hip-hop culture's mechanisms of "branding" along with its attention to organic vocabulary and grammar for expressing its ideals might serve as useful resource for those interested in extending the reach of humanism. That is to say, like hip-hop culture, humanists consider their thought and practices to be marginalized and despised; but unlike hip-hop culture this status has not resulted in the same type of global reach. Hence, humanists might ask what is it about hip-hop culture and its approach to public recognition that might be of benefit to humanists? The second chapter uses Camus and hip-hop culture to wrestle with death. It critiques theistic approaches to death for the manner in which they limit the appeal of life, and offers a humanist corrective that highlights a posture of living into death. That is to say, rather than viewing death as a problem, I use Camus and rap music to argue for an understanding of death as intimately linked to life. Hence, it, death, is not a disruption of life and cannot be marked off or isolated. It is not a problem of being. The final chapter in the volume concerns shaping public space by giving attention to the problem of theistic vocabulary and grammar as the framing of democratic ideals. It calls for greater attention to the development of a language of the public that is more expansive than theistic language allows.

The volume ends with an epilogue looping back to Camus and Sisyphus. This last element closes out the book as it started by highlighting the manner in which these three—race, religion, and cultural production—shape so much of the humanist's struggle. The question becomes, already and always, while rolling the rock of race, religion, and cultural production, can humanists think and work in ways that make it possible to imagine happiness? Something of this question shadows each chapter and comes again to the forefront in the epilogue.

SECTION ONE

Race

As numerous scholars have noted for a good number of years, race is a human preoccupation. In fact, much of the Western world has been shaped with some attention to the nature and meaning of race as a social construct that determines how groups are described, understood, addressed, and treated. At times this has been a matter of curiosity. Yet, race has also connoted difference given particular socioeconomic, political, and cultural charge. The more pernicious turn regarding this framing of "otherness" has involved the use of race to justify disregard, violence, and dehumanization. How to recognize and address the often-tragic consequences of race *qua* racism has been a source of energetic conversation and more than a few articles and books.

Oddly missing, in a meaningful way, from the vanguard of these conversations and scholarship have been humanists. This is at least my take on race and the humanist "movement." This observation is not meant to dismiss humanists but rather to express the curious absence of those who, by their very philosophy of existence, should be concerned deeply with the embodied nature of life and the need to maintain human dignity. Why not more attention to race and racism?

The pieces in this section offer a corrective to this oversight by addressing the nature of race and racism from an African American humanist perspective. I do not mean to suggest the only way to address race is by means of attention to African American experience. No, this certainly is not the case, but it is an important way—one that has a particularly prominent place in the collective imagination of the Modern West.

The chapters in this section range from general considerations to particularity. They move from what it means to be "black" and humanist, to what it means to live as an African American humanist, to how humanists might respond to the violence of racism through a case study of Trayvon Martin. It ends with an investigation of W. E. B. Du Bois.

1

Racing humanism: Two examples for context

Despite assumptions *all* African Americans are believers in god(s), there are long-standing modalities of humanism within African American communities.[1] To illustrate this claim, I offer two models, both of which involve an effort on the part of African Americans to address race within the context of human experience. Yet, while both are concerned with race (and racism) on some level, they approach it in different ways.[2]

I refer to the two models as "shadow" humanism and "naturalistic" humanism. The former involves a robust concern with human accountability and responsibility within the context of a lingering sense that there is "something" providing a logic for life—albeit a somewhat historicized "something." It might prove difficult for both theists and nontheists to appreciate my claim for this first mode of humanism because the conceptual paradigm of the "divine" or "god" remains operative. However, my argument is that there is a mode of religious expression within African American communities—with historical roots—that promotes deep regard for humanity within the world. In this instance, humans have what philosopher William R. Jones has labeled "functional ultimacy."[3] That is to say, despite all, humans have will and freedom that affords them the ability to determine the content of their lives to some significant degree. While the symbol God may in this instance serve as suggesting parameters for ethics and morality, human conduct marks the ability of humans to make determinations. Or, as my grandmother would remind, "God has no hands but your hands, no legs but your legs . . . " This pronouncement made on so many occasions speaks to a turn from a rigid metaphysics that positions

God as wholly "other." God conceptualized, as my grandmother suggests, is recognizable with any clarity only when operating within history, in the garb of human life.

The metaphysics embraced here is not atheistic in a strict sense, empirically based information matters to the extent the claims of theism and its sacred texts are measured against the advancement of life options for African Americans in historical time and space. That is to say, theistic language in this context is maintainable to the extent it describes historical developments. Faith and works are joined to the benefit of those suffering from the ramifications of race. In addition, this mode of humanism recognizes and pushes for the integrity of life over against effort to deform, reduce, and pervert life (e.g., racism). More than simple humanitarianism—the desire to do "good" so as to expand well-being—what I reference here is a shifting theological and philosophical plain whereby a sense of grounded ethics is tied to altered ways of thinking. To borrow from Henry David Thoreau's argument in *Walden*, this "slide" toward humanism involves an effort to be good (to revitalize the significance of existence within the context of history) as a precursor to doing good in/to the world.[4] I would not call this essence preceding experience, but rather a sense that for those at this point on the spectrum of theism/humanism there is a synergistic relationship between the two that is not captured sufficiently through traditional theologizing. Elsewhere I have labeled this mode of humanism—"weak" humanism, but here I suggest a different naming so as to remove negative connotations and push humanists to move beyond easy denigration of the unfamiliar.[5]

The latter, naturalistic humanism, lacks concern with divine reality of any kind (no matter how much it bends to the will of human history) and limits its focus to the significance of material life—it's strengths and shortcomings. It is more clearly nontheistic in orientation and easily recognized as consistent with the humanist principles I outlined in the introduction to this volume. Elsewhere I called this mode of humanism "strong" humanism; however, here I have changed the name so as to avoid connotations that take away from what I hope to offer as a balanced discussion—a creative tension between these two categories of humanist thought and insight.

What this chapter provides on one level is descriptive of how humanist sensibilities are expressed—more explicitly in some instances than in others. Yet, in another way, what I offer is a hermeneutical experiment—a reading of African American meaning making through the lens of human engagement. There is something heuristic about this chapter that is meant to suggest the need to carefully explore and present the dynamic relationship between race and humanism—mindful of the specificity marking how particular groups name, present, and practice humanism in light of contextual considerations. Embedded in this discussion, then, is the suggestion that humanistic sensibilities within this particular "raced" community—and I would assert in all others as well—are played out along a continuum, along a spectrum moving from nagging questions regarding certain dimensions of theistic belief(s) that serve to modify theistic sensibilities in private and perhaps in public to some degree (e.g., diminished church attendance), to a full-blown rejection of theism and all that it represents. Between these two are various modalities of disbelief. Nothing about the presence and development of humanism within lived community is neat, straightforward, and without fuzzy edges.

This is not to co-opt nor colonize *all* African American religious sensibilities and possibilities, as if to say all people are inherently humanistic despite what they might say to the contrary. (This, of course, means not utilizing a hermeneutic of intrinsic godlessness.) There are renderings of theism that are clearly outside any plausible entanglement with humanism or atheism—their theological, philosophical, and ideological disagreements to grand to think otherwise. Instead, I suggest there is bleed through when it comes to the dynamics of thought and praxis informing certain modes of liberal religion and humanism.

If one avoids a hermeneutic of Christian dominance (i.e., the United States is and has always been a Christian nation), not all that appears on the surface to be strictly theistic in a traditional sense really fits that mold. There are styles of expression, of "meaning making" that are blurred. These modes house sensibilities pointing in two directions and that are recognized (and claimed) by both theists and nontheists. (There are dimensions of President Obama's theo-ethics for instance embraced by both theists and nontheists, and I argue this is because of his adherence to the liberal social gospel.) In addition, there are certain sensibilities that are clearly godless, while others are clearly god-filled.

What I offer in this first chapter, in this brief and descriptive typology, is some sense of two points along this spectrum of humanism, with said humanism framing a response to and corrective of race/racism in African American communities.

Shadow humanism

Before offering something of an intellectual history related to this first form of humanism, another word regarding the phrasing and its intended meaning is vital. I call this "shadow" humanism because it does not fully reject Christian metaphysics, but does not embrace many elements of this metaphysics. That is to say, it, like humanism as commonly understood, premised its consideration on a concern with humanity—its wants and needs. It frames its understanding of life from the perspective of human angst and desire. Yet, it speaks of God and other forces, but in ways that often reveal their cultural importance over against any verifiable significance. That is to say, this humanism is not only shadowed by some of the stuff of theism, but it also embraces many elements of what humanists are more comfortable in recognizing as the stuff of empirically centered existence.[6]

Shadow humanism lurks in the secret meetings of enslaved Africans—the hush arbor meetings during which enslaved Christians worked through their theological positions in spirituals and sermons, over against the dominant presentation of the "Gospel" message. Even prior to the creation of institutional forms, African American Christianity presented a humanistic understanding of the intersections between the transcendent and the immanent. The spirituals, the theological language of the proto-African American church, outlined this connection by framing a robust anthropology through which and in connection to which divinity is presented. In this way humanity is recognized as a weighty reality, one through whose mark on the world God is seen and experienced. This is the significance of the *imago Dei* as found in the religious songs of the enslaved. Most importantly, this framing of the spiritual's world, this cartography of human development within the spirituals, is also the best way to map the movement of God in the world—and the cipher for this is Jesus Christ. The biblical world and the contemporary moment are brought into harmony, time and space as related to religious meaning are collapsed. In a significant way, the presence of Christ—God and humanity in perfect harmony—marks the spirituals as shadow humanism: Human struggle and existential movement as irrepressible statement of who God is and where God is found. That is to say, God is only knowable as a sign or symbol of ethical and moral correctness within the empirical arrangements of life.

The African presence in North America was over a century old before this religious ethos would take sustained and somewhat "independent" institutional form with the development of black churches. But, it is within these churches that this shadow humanism took its most explicit and celebrated form through a combining of commitment to the reality of the divine and a sense of human progress and reason. This perspective lends one way to interpret the words of Robert Pope, who writes, "Our religious creeds conform more nearly to the life and teaching of the Christ. The old idea," he continues, "that theology is stationary, while every other science is progressive is absurd and must go. As more light is turned on, this science becomes more comprehensive in its scope, more responsive to human need, and expresses more full the thought of God."[7] Even more telling than Pope's words is the perspective of Norman Brown regarding the doctrine of God.

In an article in the *AME Church Review*, Brown says, "A people's God is no bigger than their needs, no higher than their aspirations."[8] Doctrine of God is measured against anthropology. That is why Brown could write "the only God that will satisfy and that is practical is the God in you; and if you cannot find God in you, it is useless to search for him amid the stars."[9]

Prior to these statements by Pope and Brown, pronouncements in support of a type of shadow humanism were present in statements by leaders such as Bishop Henry McNeal Turner of the African Methodist Episcopal Church—the oldest African American denomination in the United States. Turner, in his most polemical style, proclaimed the blending of transcendence and immanence with the statement "God is a Negro!" By this Turner meant to counter white supremacist manipulations of doctrine of God by signifying them, turning them on their head. More importantly, this intertwining of God and humanity also points to the continuing importance of humanity for a proper understanding of reality: God is real and present in the world, and humans are accountable for acting, practicing struggle for improvement. Human growth and development is vital, a religious truth, that works in conjunction with a deep and abiding confirmation of the reality of God. The Christ Event is the primary example of how this blending of transcendence and immanence works. Hence, this style of humanism within nineteenth- and early twentieth-century black churches amounted to a weighty and persistent Christology as the centerpiece of thought and the model of historic(al) action.

The Great Migration brought this concern with a humanized Gospel and "earthy" Christology into relief in that it highlighted a debate regarding the proper orientation of black churches—"this-worldly" versus "other-worldly." The latter position has been, for the most part, downplayed within progressive churches in that it tends to represent an embrace of transcendent concerns—salvation as nonhistorical development. The former orientation, however, understands the significance of God's movement in the world in terms of historically situated transformation—the increase in life options and greater possibilities for human existence.[10]

The former was also given both explicit and implicit attention during the civil rights movement, as black churches were called, through a social Christianity posture of certain leaders, to give an account of their commitment to human progress as the hallmark of God's concern and character. In a word, churches were challenged to live out a posture of humanism that made consistent if not synonymous salvation and liberation—Christian activism and the presence of God in human history. With this posture churches, at their best, emphasized a social gospel-type synthesizing of God and history in ways that point out the humanity of God.

This shadow humanism involved a sense of the collective, communal concern with transformation over against the radical individualism of the "other-worldly" orientation. The efforts of figures such as Martin Luther King, Jr, a student of the Boston University School of Personalism and a devoted member of the Black Church Tradition, called for social transformation as the proper business of black churches. In less academic guise, activist Ella Baker expressed this perspective in plain terms and laments what she perceives as a shifting theological and ethical terrain. "My grandfather," Baker writes, "had gone into the Baptist ministry, and that was part of the quote, unquote, Christian concept of sharing with others. I went to a school that went in for Christian training. Then, there were people who 'stood for something,' as I call it. Your relationship to human beings was more important than your relationship to the amount of money that you made."[11]

This humanization of God's presence in the world takes an odd turn in the late twentieth and early twenty-first centuries through the Mega-church phenomenon and the Prosperity Gospel. The early "this-worldly" orientation involved a commitment to the Christ Event as a call for a theistic humanism devoted to both a devotion to God and a deep regard for the needs and responsibility of humanity. But the Mega-church phenomenon (through the Prosperity Gospel) *at its worst* involves disregard for the needs and responsibilities of humanity as the centerpiece of the Christ Event. Highlighted instead is a superficial appeal to the economic and social conjuring of scripture for the benefit of individuals measured in terms of material acquisition and a sacralizing of the "American Dream."[12] Even efforts at transformation often morph into bits of charity (e.g., "self-help" strategies based on slogans and pseudo-psychology) as opposed to social gospel efforts to reimagine, reconstruct, the infrastructure of social existence.

Shadow humanism within the Black Church Tradition is expressed beyond the rhetoric of civil rights through an appreciation for the physical presence of African Americans, for the beauty and value of black bodies. Martin L. King, Jr, for example, highlighted this. While racial discrimination for centuries was marked by a disregard for black bodies as of less importance and value, King's work entailed a reenvisioning of these bodies in ways that show them as beautiful, as epistemologically and ontologically "weighty." This reworking of the aesthetic of black bodies—achieved by King in speeches and the "arrangement" of bodies in direct protest— rendered them visible and therefore demanding of public consideration. King invested public discourse and action with metaphysical significance and importance. But, at the same time, he rendered the implications of metaphysical truths deeply mundane and, in the process, he celebrated highly visible black bodies as markers of intimacy between the divine and the human—an assumption already in place with respect to white bodies. This process involved, among other theological things, a radicalized theological anthropology (i.e., discussion of the nature and meaning of humanity), one that took seriously the ontological (i.e., a basic concern with the nature of being) and existential (i.e., a primary interest in experience) damage done by the socioeconomic and cultural quarantining of black bodies. One gets a sense of this liberal and "black" theological articulation of public policy in King's view of the struggle. While he will be the subject of another chapter for now I am concerned with just one particular dimension of his thought. "Christians," according to King, "are bound to recognize any passionate concern for social justice. Such concern is basic in the Christian doctrine of the Fatherhood of God and the brotherhood of man [sic]." Furthermore, he continued, "Christians are also bound to recognize the ideal of a world unity in which all barriers of caste and color are abolished. Christianity repudiates racism."[13]

The achievements marking the civil rights movement are built in part on King's rendering of a new cartography of public life, premised on the beauty/value of black bodies. Whereas poverty and other forms of discrimination marked black bodies as valueless, as unimportant, as disposable, as invisible with respect to the public arena of democratic engagement, King's civil rights work asserted the opposite: black bodies house a profound importance that must be recognized and embraced through public mechanism geared toward the fostering of "whole-ness." What King, as representative of the black church at its best, attempted to achieve through civil rights praxis involved the widespread and liberal understanding of the Christ Event through which humanity is invested with physical and spiritual (aesthetic) profoundness that must be recognized and safeguarded.

Naturalistic humanism

Not all African Americans embrace shadow humanism as their orientation toward life and thought, and the signs of this alternate framework—naturalistic humanism—run as deep as those of shadow humanism.

As some enslaved Africans sang spirituals celebrating the ontological and existential synergy between the divine and the human—best represented through the immanence of the divine in Christ—others signified this perspective and gave their full attention to humanity. This attention to humanity is the language of the blues in which metaphysical assertions are met with suspicion and immanence is of primary concern. "I used to ask God questions, then answer that question my self," as the blues tune goes.

Even the basic mode of communication between the transcendent realm and the immanent space known as human history is held suspect, and it is signified—giving priority to the demands and troubles of the existential condition of humanity: "Our father, who is in heaven, white man owe me eleven and pay me seven, they kingdom come, they will be done, and if I hadn't took that, I wouldn't had none." As these lines suggest, the blues provide a vocabulary and grammar of meaning that jettison traditional metaphysical formulations dependent on notions of the divine. In their place, these tunes advocate concern with messy business of human interaction in the world.

While the blues often involve coding of the naturalistic humanism position, enslaved African Americans who embraced this humanistic posture were not always shy about their stance. This was certainly Bishop Alexander Payne's experience when confronting a runaway slave, who questioned the existence of God: "I asked him if he was a Christian; 'no, sir,' said he, 'white men treat us so bad in Mississippi that we can't be Christians.'. . . In a word, slavery tramples the laws of the living God under its unhallowed feet-weakens and destroys the influence which those laws are calculated to exert over the mind of man; and constrains the oppressed to blaspheme the name of the Almighty."[14] Marked as it is with a triumphant sense of immanent experience as the judge of metaphysical claims, the runaway's rejection of theistic orientation of necessity involves reliance on human ingenuity and skills for the fulfillment of life.[15]

Similar sentiments to those expressed above are present in African American folktales. For instance, a Chimney sweep named John Junior rejects the supposed comfort of the Christian faith and replaces it with intense devotion to human progress and achievement based strictly on the work of human hands: "No, I ain't tendin' been' no Christian. That's the trouble with niggers now. They pray too damn much. Every time you look around you se some nigger on his knees and the white man figurin' at his desk. What in the world is they prayin' fo'? Tryin' to get to heaven? They is goin' to get there anyhow. There ain't no other Hell but this one down here. Look at me. I'm catchin' Hell right now."[16]

Naturalistic humanism in early African American communities is replaced during the twentieth century with a much firmer presentation of this perspective.[17] For instance, participation of African Americans in the communist party at times involved rejection of supernatural explanations for history, and reliance on human energy and immanence as proper orientation point to this shift. Late-twentieth-century political activities (i.e., civil rights activism) also housed this perspective. While members of the civil rights movement, as orchestrated by figures like Martin Luther King, Jr, by and large embraced traditional theism or shadow humanism, members of the Student Nonviolent Coordinating Committee (SNCC) and the Black Panther Party held a preference for the liberative possibilities of naturalistic humanism.[18]

The Harlem Renaissance also offered naturalistic humanism in various forms, but most notably in the writings of Richard Wright. The character Cross Damon from *The Outsider*, for example, limited his reach to the existential realities of a troubled and troubling world.[19] Such stories are not simply a presentation of fantastic perspectives. To the contrary, African American literary figures such as Richard Wright and James Weldon Johnson personally embraced naturalistic humanism with a certain thoughtfulness and balance. "My glance forward," Johnson wrote, "reaches no farther than this world. I admit that I throughout my life have lacked religiosity. I do not know if there is a personal God; I do not see how I can know; and I do not see how my knowing can matter. As far as I am able to peer into the inscrutable, I do not see that there is any evidence to refute those scientists and philosophers who hold that the universe is purposeless: that man, instead of being the special care of a Divine Providence, is dependent upon fortuity and his own wits for survival in the midst of blind and insensate forces."[20]

Albeit important, naturalistic humanism as presented in African American political rhetoric and literature involves a rather loose arrangement of perspectives, which do not hold the same communal weight as the organizations housing shadow humanism. Yet, this loose configuration is only one of the styles of presentation for naturalistic humanism. The UUA has for decades served as an institutional home for some African American naturalistic humanists because of its commitment to a nondoctrinal community and its resulting comfort with congregations of varying orientations. The relationship between African Americans and the UUA has involved significant rough patches, primarily revolving around issues of race relations.[21]

Nonetheless, one reason African Americans remain in the UUA in spite of cultural difficulties revolves around the manner in which the appeal to social justice is expressed in terms of human accountability and responsibility. This, within humanistic congregations, means a move away from both implicit and explicit links to notions of the transcendent and biblical notions of divine intervention that undergird the sense of liberation found in most black churches. Furthermore, even divisions of the UUA, considering themselves Christian, maintain a sense of liberation that appeals because of its commitment to "the inherent worth and dignity of every person; justice, equity and compassion in human relations," and so on.[22] In addition, the presence of African Americans in significant leadership positions, including the presidency of the Association, only serves to further enhance African American commitment to the naturalistic humanism expressed by certain segments of the UUA.[23]

Liberation in this context is similar to that proposed within shadow humanism; both are concerned with a fullness of existence, the removal of oppressive socioeconomic, political, and cultural arrangements and structures, but naturalistic humanism does not anchor this resolve in any consideration of transcendence (outside of human history), however modified, as a source for moral and ethical conduct and regulations extending outside human history.

2

African Americans living li(f)e

The first chapter worked through a typology of African American humanism and its relationship to issues of race and racism. It explored two modes of humanism, while the concern in this chapter and the rest of the volume is restricted to naturalistic or nontheistic humanism. Here I privilege nontheistic humanism in that it has received the least amount of attention and because more theistic forms of humanism are easily captured through the many publications related to liberal religion.[1] Still, this chapter builds on the first by highlighting the structuring of humanism as a response to antiblack racism in the United States. And, I begin this work with a few words on the position of African Americans in the Modern World.

Almost forty years ago, as hip-hop culture was transforming the discourse and aesthetics of urban life, as the political landscape of the United States was taking a turn away from more liberal policies couched in the hope and angst of the civil rights movement, and as the economic fortune of the nation wrestled with a posture of radical individualism, Cornel West captured the existential and ontological framing of life plaguing African Americans. "The paradox of Afro-American history," West notes, "is that Afro-Americans fully enter the modern world precisely when the postmodern period commences."[2] While intellectual energy and social vision promoted in many quarters a sense of the self as fractured, and knowledge as suspect, African Americans were pushing for (and believing themselves to have secured) a proper sense of the self as whole. And they articulated this progress through a sense of their liberation as having epistemological validity and "weight."

Such is the paradox of African American collective life in the United States. In a word, it involves tension between living a lie (i.e., structural efforts to dehumanize African Americans and have African Americans embrace that deception) and living life (i.e., constructive pushing for a robust sense of self within the context of community). African Americans—if Cornel West is correct, and I think he is—have also had good reason to question if not reject the limited sense of humanity and culturally fixed sense of "truth" marking much of modernity and its meaning frameworks.

To be African American has involved being something of an experiment or perhaps what W. E. B. Du Bois labels "a problem." Put another way, " the Negro," writes Du Bois, "is a sort of seventh son, born with a veil, and gifted with second-sight in this American world,—a world which yields him no true self-consciousness, but only lets him see himself through the revelation of the other world."[3] What Du Bois offers is a haunting depiction of the quest for meaning within the context of African American life and thought. And, of great value to this chapter, Du Bois points to the significance of cultural production for working through these deep existential questions of life in a race preoccupied context.

African American humanism

Regardless of what some say about the significance of theism within a troubled world, it is the need for life meaning within this absurd context that gives some shape to nontheistic sensibilities within African American communities. Although articulated clearly and with great power in twentieth-century African American cultural production through figures of the Harlem Renaissance and Black Realism, they were only rehearsing in their work what African Americans knew and lived for centuries. For example, one can argue with relative ease Richard Wright's viewing of the mid-twentieth century through a humanistic/atheistic lens simply echoes the relevance of nontheistic orientations for African Americans known much earlier in the blues. From early communities of enslaved Africans to the present, there has been for some a general engagement with that world without the safety net of a transhistorical protector:

> Many of the religious symbols appealed to my sensibilities and I responded to the dramatic vision of life held by the church, feeling that to live day by day with death as one's sole thought was to be so compassionately sensitive toward all life as to view all men as slowly dying, and the trembling sense of fate that welled up, sweet and melancholy, from the hymns blended

with the sense of fate that I had already caught from life. But full emotional and intellectual belief never came. Perhaps if I had caught my first sense of life from the church I would have been moved to complete acceptance, but the hymns and sermons of God came into my heart only long after my personality had been shaped and formed by unchartered conditions of life. I felt that I had in me a sense of living as deep as that which the church was trying to give me, and in the end I remained basically unaffected.[4]

Some opponents of African American humanism might grumble it is merely a negative posture—one that marks denouncement of long-held values without a positive alternative in place. The assumption undergirding this critique entails a view of anything shy of a teleological informed framing of history as nihilistic, and thereby devoid of redeeming value. However, honest attention to African American humanism will point out its positive characteristics buttressing a robust commitment to embodied life. And what is more, African American humanism places the historical arrangement of life at the center of all thought and action.

A cautionary note is vital here: this is not simply the exultation of the human as the center of all existence in that African American humanism is too aware of the dangers behind this type of imbalanced anthropology.

African American humanism understands an unchecked anthropology of progress as intimately connected to the dynamics of white supremacy, sexism, homophobia, environmental destruction, and so on. In an effort to fight these types of oppression African American humanism at its best (as advocated by figures such as Alice Walker and Zora Neale Hurston) promotes the integrity of life in more general, but still material and historical, terms as the focus of humanist praxis. In this manner, African American humanism seeks to promote a sense of the individual within the context of "community" writ large.

African American humanism values a historicist perspective in a robust and sustained manner, whereby cultural and social context is given deep importance and reliance on external or fixed "Truth" is rejected. Or, as Frederick Douglass noted so long ago, appeals to the transhistorical proved fruitless in that "I prayed for emancipation for twenty years but received no answer till I prayed with my legs."[5] Amen! Of course, a secular amen.

What humanism means for African Americans

While always present in African American communities—both lodged in a general regard for the significance of human life and in a more explicit set of humanist principles played out in various ways—nontheistic postures toward the world have become more explicit.

Recent studies note an increase in the number of US citizens who publicly label themselves "Nones," growing to represent more than 10 percent of the total US population. A major point of growth within this population involves African Americans: marked by a shift from 6 percent of African Americans responding to the question of religious affiliation with "none" to over 10 percent in more recent years.[6]

I believe it safe to assume some of this growth stems from a failure on the part of theistic traditions to produce the benefits and outcome claimed as part of their teachings. Hence, it is a rejection of theism in light of persisting dilemmas and theological conservatism that fail to capture the mood and needs of so many African Americans. But this latter reason for growth is insufficient. Can nontheists really afford to simply be appreciated through negation—what other life orientations do not provide?

While the shortcomings of theistic traditions may continue to result in greater attention to and embrace of nontheistic possibilities, the value of African American humanism as a mode of thought and praxis requires something more proactive. The touting of human responsibility and accountability has to be matched by strategies for using this human-centered perspective to improve sociopolitical and economic conditions. Claims to more reasonable approaches to life, ones that explode the claims of theistic faith are insufficient when they do not have felt consequences within the lived arrangements of life. One can get a sense, a hint, of this demand for both epistemological depth and praxis in the "African Americans for Humanism" organization's self-description. And for effect, I quote at length:

> The need for critical thinking skills and a humanistic outlook in our world is great. This is no less true in the Black community than in others. Many African Americans have been engulfed by religious irrationality, conned by self-serving "faith healers," and swayed by dogmatic revisionist historians. Many others, however, have escaped the oppression of such delusions, and live happy and upstanding lives free of superstition. African Americans for Humanism (AAH) exists to bring these secular humanists together, to provide a forum for communication, and to facilitate coordinated action. In an irrational world, those who stand for reason must stand together.[7]

This critique couched in a call for more involvement and relevance entails a dichotomy of significance in that it is both a call to *and* critique of African American humanists and the larger humanist movement.

For the former, it is more comfortable to simply point a finger and wag it at the insensitive and often misguided "Movement." Yet, the situation is more complex than that and it demands African American humanists be proactive as well. A positive future shaped by growth and relevance demands the visibility of African American humanists. And strategies useful in the promotion of a viable future for African American humanism might include the following:

1. Increased production of reader-friendly materials (traditional publications and online) discussing the nature and meaning of African American humanism. Connected to this is the development of a national network of reading groups and book clubs related to humanist books;

2. Solidifying of organizations by and for African American humanism, and this means constraint on the tendency toward isolation and individualism for the sake of collective, organizational structures and processes;

3. Partnerships with organizations (including religious organizations) that are committed to sociopolitical and economic advancement based on a progressive vision. It is not necessary to create all new mechanisms for this work. In fact, the ability of African American humanists to partner on pressing issues provides greater visibility and deeper understanding of humanism as entailing more than negation;

4. Aggressive branding (to be sure, a dirty word for many) strategies. Some may find this troubling, but the future success and recognition of African American humanism must involve concerted effort to establish its "brand" potential—to establish its uniqueness and importance. All of the above play a role in this branding process;

5. Establishment of an African American Humanism Fund (not associated with a particular humanist organization) used to support and encourage humanism-based activities and promotions on the local level;

6. Connected to the issue of branding, the development of a clear and concise mission statement for the African American humanist "movement" that provides a positive and proactive stance.

The above could play a profitable role in the enhancement and growth of humanism within African American communities. However, there is a larger context, a more expansive geography of humanism to consider.

The question is this: where do African American humanists fit in the larger *tradition(s)* of American humanism?

Put differently, there is a growing awareness of and interest in humanism within the United States. We have not approached Sweden's appreciation for this orientation, yet there has been noteworthy growth.[8] Continued advancement by humanists, however, requires more attention to the significance of humanists within communities of "color" including African American communities. Even within humanist and atheist circles where there is at least the "shadow" presence of African Americans, we tend to simply call the roll of grand humanists who have maintained the tradition.

As I have stated elsewhere and on numerous occasions, this recognition of legacy is vital, but I propose digging deeper and more fully expressing the sensibilities of a human orientation painstakingly implied by African American humanists and their nontheistic ancestors. Rather than simply acknowledging the diversity, take the next step and make diversity—difference—the hallmark of humanist movements, a core value without which these movements and the organizations comprising them fail to live out the best of the humanist tradition and agenda.[9] Diversity within humanist movements is not simply a point of pride—when done moderately well—or a moment of lament without traction and without a clear call to action. It is instead the very nature of the humanist movement at its best.

3

The ongoing challenge of race

The first chapter in this section outlined the presence of humanism within African American communities as a way of "filtering" humanism through the lens of race and the type of existential and ontological questions prompted by race and racism. And, the second provided a way to think about what it means to live humanism within African American communities. This chapter takes a different turn by exploring the manner in which race shapes perceptions of how bodies occupy time and space. It goes further to interrogate the consequences of embodied black bodies being perceived as a threat, and it does so by turning to a graphic and violent example.[1] What does race mean to humanists, and what should it mean in light of its ongoing, and at times deadly, importance in US life?

Some readers may remember this report from *The New York Times* or other media outlets:

> On Feb. 26, 2012, Trayvon Martin was shot and killed by Mr. Zimmerman, a crime watch volunteer in a gated community in Sanford, Fla. The death of the unarmed black teenager and the decision of the local police not to bring charges against Mr. Zimmerman, who is Hispanic, set off a national outcry, leading the Justice Department in March to open an investigation. Trayvon, 17, was shot as he was walking to the home of his father's girlfriend from a convenience store in Sanford, just north of Orlando. Mr. Zimmerman told the police that he shot Trayvon in self-defense.[2]

George Zimmerman went on trial for the murder of Martin and ended up facing no jail time.

Media attention moved on to other tragedies. Yet, for those close to Martin, the anxiety and pain remained fresh: Trayvon Martin, 17, is dead. The bullet from the gun held by George Zimmerman, a self-appointed neighborhood watch captain, was the direct cause of this senseless death. But, the environment in which such madness could take place, an environment in which some easily assume Martin must have been the aggressor—because his black face was shrouded by a "hoodie," and his body was located outside of what was considered its proper space—has been perfected over the course of centuries.

A society in which Trayvon Martin could be perceived as out of place within his community takes its ideology and ethics from an old system of property, in which black bodies were to be monitored, rendered docile, and controlled. This old system worked based on the logic that black bodies were dangerous bodies and how they occupied space had to be watched closely. In a word, the system of slavery—the Atlantic slave trade—required a particular understanding of black bodies that continues to inform social interactions in the twenty-first century.

Humans built the slave system, developed the antiblack racism policies that undergird so many contemporary interactions, and justified both. This reality—the senseless death of Martin and the larger ideology that informed it—one might think, would temper perceptions of human nature and potential. In light of this madness, on what is human optimism built?

Many humanists and theists share a hyper-optimism regarding human progress. While each group points to the demise of the other as a key component in positive human development—both also presume proper posture toward the world, and use of a certain set of tools, to promote human advancement. For the theists this is all guided by the good intentions and assistance of a benevolent deity, and for the naturalistic humanist it is premised on the reliability of scientific inquiry and reason.

While something of a hopeful outlook is a useful approach to ethical conduct, it should be guided and monitored by a sense of realism—recognition of persistent human misconduct and the resulting moral and ethical challenges. Theists can always haul such problems to the altar, pray about them, ritualize them, or chalk them up to mystery. For the humanist, the resolution is not so easily achieved because the difficulty is not mystical. It stems from a lack of acute attention to the cultural worlds in which we live, worlds that are not so easily unpacked and addressed through appeal to science and logic. Cultural signs and symbols, cultural framings of life, and life meaning are not necessarily guided by scientific method and do not necessarily respond to reason. What is reasonable about racism? Instead they function by means of both logic and illogic. Mindful of this, a few questions should be asked:

1   What is a proper humanist response to moral failure?
2   What is the proper ethical posture toward human problems that seem to defy reason and logic?
3   In light of recent developments, do humanists understand and care about black bodies?

The tenacious nature of these questions holds relevance in that they bind together history and contemporary developments. Early moral failures shadow recent and tragic events. What I have in mind is enslavement of Africans and the sociopolitical advances the system of slavery meant for peoples of European descent. And, this framing of black bodies buttresses the murder of Trayvon Martin, in Florida. Put differently, to understand situations such as the killing of Martin, one must understand the sociopolitical, economic, and cultural legacy of the slave trade. The relevance of humanism in a diverse world depends on its ability to acknowledge and tackle such perplexing problems.

As the descendant of enslaved Africans brought to the American hemisphere, I have in mind something much larger than an individualization of this transnational problem. I see this as an educable moment—an opportunity to think deeply about the underlying issues girding a long debate concerning some very important things such as: (1) the nature of privilege within environments of discrimination; (2) the limits of individual accountability within global systems; (3) the measure of collective obligation for redress of wrongs done; and (4) the disregard of black bodies made possible through these other issues. And, turning back to the context of humanism, these issues point to a strong need for humanists to develop new frameworks for ethical thinking and praxis in often-absurd cultural worlds.

A bit of context

So much of the look, the tone and texture, the dynamics of human relationships is premised on the mechanics, policies, and infrastructures created to maintain a lucrative trade in human flesh. The more graphic signs of this situation on both sides of the Atlantic have faded with time, and the gains made by means of this extreme servitude have been filtered through economic structures that no longer bare the explicit language and signs of free black labor. As a result there is a type of forgetfulness, or a systemic failure to recognize the persistent damage done to the descendants of enslaved Africans even within the contemporary moment. The Atlantic slave trade gave way to more nuanced forms of discrimination meant to safeguard white supremacy and the sociopolitical, economic, and cultural benefits of said supremacy. While the look of these alternate mechanisms for maintaining the status quo differ from country to country, undergirding each former slaveholding country's strategies has been a discourse of "otherness" that caste those of African descent as different, insignificant, and unworthy of full participation in the life (and benefits) of that nation.

The signs of this strategy are evident: in locations on both sides of the Atlantic there have been violent and ritualized ways to keep people of African descent on the margins of collective life—lynching in the United States is one example, the murder of Martin is another.

The benefits of race-based discrimination are too great to surrender without an aggressive effort to maintain them. Yet, these more graphic models of social control were matched by more subtly presented efforts—for example, depictions of people of African descent as lacking aesthetic value; charges that black men are aggressive and a threat to the security of society (the perception of Trayvon Martin?); black women are sexually available; people of African descent are genetically inferior, and so on. The rationale for this process became normalized, and became a dimension of public and private discourse that no longer required direct articulation of white supremacy in order to justify the practices meant to safeguard inequality. Violence served as a tool of reenforcement, a way to periodically fine-tune the system of discrimination by making certain the bodies (and desires) of people of African descent remained consistent with the needs of the dominant population. Although no longer requiring direct appeal, these patterns of discrimination and their justifications framed the dynamics of life—offered restrictions on what the descents of slaves could and could not do, where they could be and where they should not be, and so on. This was understood to be correct and reasonable in that their inferior position was assumed and the consequences of inherent difference understood as negative. And so, it became a part of the metanarrative of national (international?) existence. The genius of this discrimination is the lifting of any type of moral burden and the maintenance of privileges for those of European descent that need not be spoken but are acted out in a variety of ways. Soft forms of privilege, certain assumptions that are made concerning human worth and opportunities that are based on antiblack racism forged as part of the rationale for the slave system, continue to disadvantage certain populations. Examples of the success of certain persons of African descent—keen examples such as President Obama—do not challenge this system of discrimination and white privilege, but instead reenforce it. The system requires some "exceptions" to the rule in order to validate the system as equal and advancement available to any who are willing to play by the rules and work hard. Some have seen through this system, found its cracks, and are exposing it.

Challenging the status quo: Target one—religion

At least in indirect ways, humanist activity has engaged the dynamics of discrimination (as awkward as they can be with respect to issues of diversity) with soft references to the type of religion-sanctioned trauma represented by the Atlantic slave trade. This critique includes, but extends beyond, the effort of religious organizations to build worlds based on superstition, illusions, and poor reasoning. The indictment also includes exposure of religion's intimate links to the most graphic atrocities in human history—including providing theological grounding and sanction for slavery. The slave trade needed a theological and philosophical rationale that could mask a brutality and economic agenda. And, drawing from the biblical text—things such as the Book of Genesis curse on Ham (actually on his son, Canaan) by means of which his descendants were divinely appointed servants through all generations—the subjugation of Africans was read into salvation history. Theists followed this with appeals to the New Testament, where Paul encourages a slave to return to his servitude. It does not take much investigating to know the Bible does not condemn slavery. Instead, it simply presents a narrative concerning who can be enslaved rightly. Negative color symbolism in the Bible (i.e., white as "pure" and "good," and black as "evil" and "bad") was highlighted and mapped on black bodies, rendering those bodies problematic and in need of control. In addition to this theologizing of enslavement, it was also the case that religious outfits used the rhetoric of conversion to cover economic and political desire: they would enslave Africans but reward them with spiritual (but not physical!) freedom. Churches owned slaves, preachers owned slaves, and both comforted traders with affirmations that God was on their side and favored them over their African laborers. This is all true, and there is not much new in making this important critique.

Yet, there is a general logic of difference as negative that undergirds theism in more general terms. That is to say, outside the trail of documents, sermons, pronouncements, and physical involvement on the part of religious organizations in the slave trade, theism in general—not just Christianity—tends to establish an "in" group and an "out" group. The "in" group is favored by God/gods, and those in the other group exist outside the safety of divine favor. Here is the rub: the "in" group makes use of its religious and theological lexicon to construct justifications for the marginalization and at times brutalization of outsiders. So beyond the example of the African slave trade, the Holocaust, etc., there is an inherent logic within theism making possible (when it does not actively promote) difference as a negative addressed through dehumanization and destruction.

Humanists are correct to point out the destructive qualities of religion—its unavoidable failures. But, all too often it is assumed this critique is the end of the obligation to the production of a transformed society.

Challenging the status quo: Target two—nontheist introspection

Although nontheists of all sorts are free from participation in this particular type of justification for violence and discrimination, nontheists had better exercise a modicum of humility in that one need not have God or gods in order to sanction oppression. The godless play a role in the fostering of dehumanizing practices and policies. This, in the long run, is not a matter of particular ideological drive or theological orientation, but rather dehumanization stems from deeply human inclinations and desires. And, these are just as easily sanctioned through manipulations of reason and science—that is, phrenology—as they are by divine (but illusionary) forces.

There is enough blame to go around; accountability and responsibility for the cultural worlds in which we live are not restricted to particular communities of thought. It is safe to assert that the infrastructure of enslavement and the benefits of this perpetual servitude were supported by theists and nontheists alike—just as both worked to end this tragic period of human history. If nontheists are to claim Thomas Jefferson as proponent of their more secular inclinations, his participation in the dehumanization of Africans must also be noted.

Where does this leave us? Well, shouting "I am not religious!" does little to address the ethical and moral obligations facing us all; and, it does little to destroy the delusional perspectives of the traditionally religious. Theistic or not—with respect to ethics and morals—it is a distinction without a difference.

Why do I say this? First, humanists, as I will note throughout numerous of the chapters in this volume, tend to be rather passive with respect to the defining of certain terms, like religion. Too quickly, they surrender vocabulary such as "religion" to the theists—as if the idea of "binding together" can only serve as a useful component of a theistic lexicon, and a fundamentalist theism at that. I am one who argues religion can be understood as a descriptive term meant to capture the human push to make life meaningful. That is to say, as I will note regularly in this volume, it is a hermeneutic by means of which human experience (just mundane human experience) is mined for what it says about our response to the deepest existential and ontological challenges we face. There is no requirement of God or gods in this definition and it is just as plausible as any other. Religion need not be *sui generis*; it can easily and simply serve as a way of naming human experience—not sacred experience, but simply human experience that revolves around our effort to wrestle with the significant questions of our existence on planet earth.

Does this mean humanists *must* understand themselves as "religious"? No. I am simply saying humanists should be more intentional regarding the development of their lexicon. Yet, my claim will disturb many of my humanist friends. I have heard the laments and complaints before. Nonetheless, I insist such thinking is not pandering to theists; it is not conformist; nor is it a matter of accommodation. Rather, it is an effort to provide tropes or signifiers that help capture the human process of living within the context of human history—nothing supernatural or mystical about this.[3]

One should not assume that theists are the only ones who get to define and own terminology. In fact, a demand to rethink religious vocabulary might serve to damage some of the assumed integrity of theistic worldviews by removing the illusory cosmic underpinning of their lexicon. This challenge might also remove some of the nonsensical justification for discrimination supported by that lexicon. But this work must not serve as a distraction; in a word, it does not justify humanists failing to take an inventory of their participation in discourses and actions marked by racial discrimination.

Moral obligation to address wrongs of the past is paramount and incumbent upon all. The demand for an ethical posture toward the world and corresponding activity is also incumbent on all. With respect to the continuing trauma resulting from centuries of slavery, this requires something nations have been reluctant to provide. Attacks on the logic of discrimination have over the course of a good number of years been matched by demands for an apology for slavery and for reparations. An apology, and payment . . . yes.

As Robert Beckford points out in his brilliant BBC documentary titled "The Empire Pays Back," (2006), the economic gains of slavery over the course of centuries amount to trillions of pounds in the United Kingdom, and the situation is not dissimilar in the United States. An apology has been difficult to come by in both countries, and reparations have been an even more charged and divisive topic. Yet, neither is foreign; nations have apologized for moral failures and unforgivable violence such as the Holocaust and the internment camps in the United States.

These apologies have been matched in many cases with economic resource meant to make up some of the gap in healthy life options and stable infrastructures forced by violence and death encountered. Why not the same for people of African descent? This is a charged question, *and* it is a good question. Some argue the reluctance to provide financial recompense stems from the types of memory loss noted above: because it was so long ago, how do we know who has benefited? Why should those who did not directly enslave anyone lose out on resource (and privileges) because of the sins of others? And, how would money even be distributed to the descents of slaves?

Do I believe financial compensation is required? *Yes*. It would speak to moral centering, recognition of humanity violated, and the making visible of what has been hidden. Only in this way can productive conversation take place. Only in this way can a nation's moral compass be reset in ways that make real its rhetoric of democracy and citizenship.

Sharing resources allows for the development of new infrastructures providing opportunities and points of access for those who have been disadvantaged. Here is my angle on this: I think individuals are accountable for acknowledging and troubling privileges connected to race-based discrimination (i.e., the residue of the slave system). In addition, individuals should work to destroy the mechanism of race-based advantages that disadvantage so many, and this can be done through moral and ethical commitment to justice work.

In addition to individuals, there are systemic dimensions of the problem that must be addressed. And systemic problems require systemic solutions. So, rather than simply attacking individuals, I prefer—as Beckford does in his documentary—to target the national and transnational corporations and corporate interests that house the vast majority of the wealth tainted with the blood of Africans. The legacy of the slave trade is most graphic on the level of the collective. To simply target individuals might provide emotional release, a psychic corrective; but there are limited benefits to this. Again, this is not to demise the microsigns of slave-based wealth. Individuals are accountable. However, it is important to also recognize that slavery was a national and transnational problem and the full and sustained resolution must be mindful of this fact.

To carry this forward, reparations should be arranged not in terms of individual payments, but instead through the development of institutions, programs, and other structures offering assistance with the correcting of disadvantages enslavement produced over centuries. Think in terms of educational opportunities, job training and employment programs, political power through paid lobbyists, archives, museums, and galleries that preserve and house the cultural production of people of African descent, resources to fight the "New Jim Crow" as Michelle Alexander names the racially biased criminal "justice" system, media outlets to advance the interests of people of African descent within popular imagination, and so on.[4] These collective resources would then be available to descents of slaves based on need and desire. Who pays for this? The answer: transnational corporations of all sorts and governments based on profits for the former and dedicated budget lines (and policies) for the latter.

Issues of apologies and monetary recompense aside, debates regarding the Atlantic slave trade and its contemporary implications point out other flaws. For instance, the lack of critical thinking skills, and a reluctance to know and process history have done deep damage. Generations continue to emerge that think and behave without clear understandings of context, without even an interest in investigation and rigorous debate. *A few sound bites, a few catch phrases—that's it.* Here is the issue: rather than lamenting or mocking this ignorance, humanists of all sorts might spend more time developing creative strategies that address such shortcomings. This, of course, requires more than tirades against ignorant theists and destructive religions. Deconstruction of flawed patterns of thought is vital, but this must be matched by constructive efforts beyond the "usual suspects."

The implications

Humanists need to branch out beyond insulated conversations at private meetings and gatherings. Why not, for example, work with some of the students in some of the more challenged grade schools and high schools? Sponsor activities that foster critical thinking skills, effective communication strategies, and models of leadership that are organic? Encourage the development of critical thinkers who can interrogate and unpack superstitions of all sorts—whether they are religious, political, economic, or social? This approach may not receive the same media attention as attacks on the religious, but its impact is long term because it nurtures citizens who have the skills necessary to cut through the crap of our cultural worlds.

I suggest this approach of working backward and advancing critical thinking skills over mere deconstruction of traditional theism(s) because theisms and their theological underpinnings mutate, morph, and transform. This is certainly one way to think about the growth in the Prosperity Gospel and the megachurches associated with it. Do these really indicate the vulnerability (let alone death) of "religion"?

If humanist organizations and groups are already doing this sort of work, good for them. But until this is a national and transnational strategy understood as basic to secular core values, the impact will be minimal.

Doing the work I am proposing means moving beyond the already "converted." The effort is not necessarily to convert these young people to humanism—but simply to promote the skills necessary to think critically, in light of good information. This involves strategies that touch this population in creative and imaginative ways—something along the lines of "engaged learning" strategies through multiple outlets of application and practice. Who knows, this approach might also become a way to address issues of diversity within nontheistic movements and organizations.

I want to believe that the development of engaged and critical thinkers, who have the communication skills and innovative processes of application, is more important than limited and limiting commitment to the destruction of religion.

Controlling of theistic religion might be aided through traditional means of approach—intellectual critique, practical activism, public policy debate, and lobby. However, to be really effective requires the participation of more than just public nontheists (e.g., atheists and humanists). It requires an informed citizenry, and we produce this—again—through more constructive efforts to enhance critical thinking skills, effective communication strategies, and innovative models of leadership within populations least likely to attend rallies, conferences, and conventions—grade school children, high school children . . . young people. That is to say, apply humanist values and offer insights in a broad manner by working to enhance the skills necessary to interrogate theological and ideological assumptions, to question sacred pronouncements in light of lived circumstances and felt human need. Critiquing fundamentalism in any of its incarnations and promoting models of collective living that nurture our best attributes and stifle our most harmful tendencies should be the goal. Making progress on this front would be a victory.

Doing this work does not necessitate a pledge of atheism, but instead demands the type of good thinking hygiene and perspective we might be well positioned to provide. In a word, we might want to focus more aggressively on cutting theism off at its source, deny it vulnerable minds upon which to feed, and do so by fostering generations with the capacity for clear and reasonable thought. This is not the same direct attack on religious nonsense. Theists have come to expect that, but instead it stems the tide of adherents through organized efforts by humanism-informed critical thinking skills, effective communication techniques, and innovative models of application aimed at addressing pressing issues and problems—for example, theism's influence on public discourse—of our day.

Over time a citizenry develops with the capacity to think, to challenge, to ask questions—and in this way to appreciate the importance attached to creating reasonable societies marked by an ever-decreasing level of racial intolerance and violence. And, whether or not these free thinkers label themselves atheists, or humanists, or not, they have the capacity to serve as allies and they have the skills necessary to limit the unreasonable assertion of theistic religion perspective and opinions in the public arena. And they do so not necessarily because they claim the label of atheist or humanist, but because development of a more secular and less racist society makes good sense.

This development of an informed and thinking citizenry might not put an end to senseless murder, to disregard for the well-being of "others," but it does provide a way of interrogating and hopefully controlling and deconstructing our worst, human inclinations. Progress on this front—dismantling the structures and ideologies that nurture dehumanization—would be a fitting response by humanists to the murder of Trayvon Martin, and the many other tragic acts of violence against black bodies.

4

Does race have a religion? On the "Faith" of Du Bois

Long after his death, scholars and a more general readership find W. E. B. Du Bois' writings compelling, and continue to respond to his framings of our social worlds.[1] His mapping of race as the dominant cultural paradigm of the twentieth century spoke to the texture of these discursive and material worlds, and provided a basis for ongoing ideological battles and justice-based activism. Furthermore, the vocabulary and grammar Du Bois used at times while explaining the human response to these constructed worlds has promoted consideration of religion's role in the development of these sociocultural worlds as well as its place in efforts to reconstruct them along more democratic lines. Not content to analyze what he argues when using religion as a conceptual framework, some scholars have at least in passing remarked on his personal relationship to theistic faith.

Having provided commentary in the previous chapter regarding how race/racism lives and what it allows vis-à-vis Trayvon Martin, in this chapter I use attention to Du Bois's personal faith stance (or lack thereof) as a way to interrogate assumed connections between race and religion in a general sense. But, more to the point, this concern with Du Bois also sheds light on the tendency to assume those who study religion or work with religious language are of necessity theistic. Using Du Bois as something of a case study, it is possible to also secure greater clarity regarding how humanists might work with religious language—a mode of poetic language—for addressing cultural worlds without being consumed by theism. If Du Bois could use religious language to unpack race while maintaining at the very least an ambiguous relationship to theism, why cannot humanists?

Religion and Du Bois: Friends or enemies?

While Du Bois provides clues, it is far from easy to decipher with any certainty what he believed and endorsed on a personal level. We are no closer to closure on this issue, and in fact questions abound for those within the academic study of religion.

At times he approached religion with a degree of disinterest, as a matter of intellectual and political dissection, and then there are his "prayers," etc. What about Du Bois' particular efforts and goals that required this opaque approach to religiosity? Was it a sense of privacy—a desire to avoid having readers and listeners assess his thought simply based on his personal relationship to the religious history of African Americans? Here I work through these questions by giving attention to books recently published on the question of Du Bois and religion. The authors are Edward Blum, Jonathon Kahn, and Terrence Johnson.

Undergirding these three books (*An American Prophet, Divine Discontent,* and *Tragic Soul-Life*) is a bit of speculation regarding this religious opacity, and some effort to provide new insight beginning with a type of historiography of Du Bois's religiosity. As readers discover, some scholars argue Du Bois moved away from any personal allegiance to theism over the course of his years—instead critiquing organized religion and advocating for reason and scientific investigation as grounding for a more material-based perception of life. In making this argument, scholars have labeled Du Bois an agnostic, skeptic, or an atheist. Du Bois's writings, therefore, are read as a critique of theism—a dismantling of its assumed meaning in ways that prevent it being reestablished. Therefore, the argument goes, Du Bois does not embrace theism through his use of religious language and grammar, but rather troubles it as one who knows it from a growing distance. Perhaps a critique is sometimes a matter of forging distance as opposed to suggesting an alternate style of embrace? Perhaps for Du Bois the very embodiment of African Americans, the recognition of their materiality, and the celebration of their vitality and importance replace theism? Other scholars suggest Du Bois was a Christian—a man of theistic faith and commitment—albeit far from a traditional type of Christian. The man who painted such compelling portraits of the world through his words, and who outlined in such a haunting fashion the nature of race in the United States, discussed his personal orientation in such a manner as to foster these divergent opinions.

The books discussed here mirror a similar range of opinions.[2] All three authors agree Du Bois provides important commentary on and analysis of religion in African American communities, and does so in ways that shed light on the nature and meaning of individual and collective life—including the function of race and the nature of democratic engagement. For all three the use of religious vocabulary and grammar is important, but they tend to disagree as to what it says about Du Bois as a man of "faith." However, they share a conviction that scholars like award-winning David Levering Lewis have it wrong: Du Bois was not dismissive of theism, nor was he an atheist without any regard for issues of religious belief. Even a more moderate position such as humanist (qualified in a variety of ways—religious, secular, and so on) fails to receive mention as a viable alternative by these three authors, although it could certainly capture much of what each has in mind. Furthermore, two of the three are critical of scholars like the late award-winning Manning Marable, who argued Du Bois was a man of faith— something akin to traditional African American Christianity. Instead, Edward Blum argues Du Bois embraced a creative and earthy form of Christian faith—a belief system radically different than traditional African American Christianity. Jonathon Kahn suggests Du Bois held to a version of religious naturalism informed by Pragmatism. And, Terrence Johnson reads Du Bois as an exemplar of moral thinking whose "religious" sensibilities are informed by an array of transatlantic religious orientations, but with a decidedly Christian perspective. Each gives careful attention to the development in Du Bois of a particular modality of religiosity, although doing so is not the primary concern for writing. To the contrary, this information functions as contextual material useful in understanding the importance of religion to Du Bois' as well as his use of religion as conceptual tool.

Beyond their larger arguments, what leaps out as important is the underlying paradox tied to the manner in which the nature of religion as private mechanism of meaning and public vehicle for transformation rest so heavily on the shoulders of a thinker and activist whose own relationship to theism seems so uncertain.

What is at stake? Why depend so heavily on Du Bois to give shape to contemporary understandings of the nature, meaning, and function of the religious?

A prophet's new Christianity

For Blum, Du Bois provides a keen sense of how religion (in the form of theism) functions as a personal *and* public device for envisioning and enacting praxis capable of addressing the country's past and present relationship to difference. The book is as concerned with a historical and intellectual apology for faith in the public arena as it is with clarifying the muddy discussion of Du Bois' personal engagement with Christianity. This corrective, Blum notes, addresses the manner in which long-standing flawed interpretations based on secondary materials as opposed to close readings of Du Bois's actual writings have tainted perspective on his relationship to theism.

Tackling religion within the various genres of Du Bois writings is something of an archeological venture meant to surface a different Du Bois—one who held to a version of theistic faith and whose writings on the topic shed light useful in transforming the contemporary world through—rather over against—theistic faith.

Blum goes even further to say discussion of a shift from religious suspicion to atheism better represents the posture of the Academy toward religion than it does Du Bois's feelings. Still, not even Blum can deny what seems a growing agnosticism in Du Bois's writings; however, he is vehement in his denial that this is a form of atheism at its core or that it suggests a decreased importance given theism in his writings. He does not deny Du Bois often came across as opposed to theism, but he highlights Du Bois's series of prayers and meditations as providing a spiritual grounding for material activities; and his writings on the Black Church Tradition point to more than academic curiosity. There is no doubt but that critique of churches does not constitute atheism per se. But it is also the case that use of theological language does not prove theistic commitment. Nonetheless, for Blum, Du Bois's use of religious-theological vocabulary and images can be taken as a somewhat literal indication of his personal engagement with theistic faith. He uses them not simply because they are available to him or familiar to his audience but because they speak to a certain type of personal importance and meaning. He was a religious thinker, something of a prophet (as the subtitle of the book makes clear—" . . . *American Prophet*"). What remained of faith, Blum would have readers understand, was that which could withstand the probing of science, the strictures of reason, and the context of the material world of experience. It is Du Bois calling for the death of old religion and the birth of a new mode of earthy faith embodied and redemptive. As Blum reads him, Du Bois provides a link between the best of the social gospel tradition and more aggressive theological frameworks represented by liberation theologies in the United States such as black theology that understands the Gospel to call for justice based on its recognition of God siding with the oppressed.[3]

Du Bois's growing materialism does not pose a problem, for Blum, but rather demonstrates the various framings of life to which theistic articulations of meaning can be applied. Religion can do many types of work—safeguarding discrimination and dismantling the cosmic justifications for it in ways that make it approachable through secular means. And so, like many before and after him, Du Bois worked to dismantle religious justifications for racism by disrupting traditional notions of a God working in the world who sanctioned discrimination and whose motives cannot be questioned. He signified modalities of faith that sanction injustice by casting despised African Americans in the most significant of religious roles—for example, transfigurations of Christ as an embodied African American.

Blum advances the plasticity of faith in order to keep Du Bois within theism's assembly—the "cloud of witnesses." Tension and paradox became the friends of theism, whereby Du Bois "was both 'orthodox' and 'not orthodox at all'." "He," Blum continues, "was a church reformer who rarely attended church. He was a priest with no church, a prophet who presented his works as history, sociology, and fiction." (59) The sacred and secular become somewhat indistinguishable, and perhaps it is for this reason Blum argues Du Bois has a connection to twentieth-century liberation theology. That mode of socially minded theological discourse—for example, black theology and womanist theology—works to bring religious identity in line with activism in such a way as to render religious commitment and public obligation the same. And, in the process ground the divine in the mundane such as James Cone does in arguing God is ontologically black. Spirituality for Blum's Du Bois is a matter of depth of engagement and commitment as opposed to the signpost of connection to a realm beyond the reach of reason and materiality. Du Bois offers a reframing, a remaking of the Christian faith, that strips away layers of compromise with sociopolitical and economic corruption. In this way he establishes renewed potential of theistic faith to speak with clarity and force to the pressing issues of his day and ours. He is, as Blum proclaims late in the book, a "religious modernist." (160) What Blum means by this label is not clear, but one can assume it might entail a figure whose theistic religiosity is responsive to embodied life, who advances secular knowledge, and who is committed to religious meaning responsive to the issues of modern social existence. Such a religious orientation is more than a form of civic religion. Instead, it is a deep faith that acknowledges the power of theistic signs and symbols, while denying the more deeply supernatural and magical covering that has chocked theism for far too long.

Blum's sense of Christianity gives it a type of Kevlar wrapping whereby it remains flexible, but the covering prevents it from succumbing to any deep damage. Even the "atheism" of Du Bois amounts to only the emergence of a new and more limber Christianity (180)—a religion with a lean set of "metaphors" and "symbolic principles." (198) This new Christianity is perhaps akin to what figures such as Dietrich Bonheoffer and Howard Thurman would understand as the teachings of Jesus the Christ over against the gospel of the organized churches tainted by sociopolitical and economic considerations.[4] Within this new Christianity, Du Bois is religious teacher standing in the lineage of figures such as Jesus the Christ (200), but proclaiming a gospel to challenge racial discrimination. In short, according to Blum's Du Bois, theistic religion matters in identity formation and social development. The "color line" marking the twentieth century is buttressed by religious ideals and sentiments. We, Blum advises, have much to learn across disciplines from Du Bois perspective on theistic faith, and to do otherwise is to taint the content and purpose of Du Bois's work by removing its spiritual, its religious tone, texture, and internal structuring.

Black life through religious naturalism

In a step away from Blum's book, Kahn argues he is not concerned primarily with identifying Du Bois as religious in any particular manner, but rather he is concerned with what *informs* Du Bois's use of religion as well as *how* Du Bois uses religion in his writings. Mindful of this, he begins *Divine Discontent* by establishing intellectual and literary space for his assessment of Du Bois. Kahn seeks to present a corrective to secondary literature that paints Du Bois as antireligion, as against religion in any shape or form. But he offers a word of caution against going too far in the other direction, and so labeling Du Bois a Christian and reading his popular and academic writings in this light is to miss Du Bois' transformation of Pragmatism into an African American approach to life. Not a Christian, not an atheist, but rather a pragmatist.[5]

Du Bois's religiosity is more akin to a pragmatic religious naturalism—informed by William James, John Dewey, and George Santayana. Based on these figures Kahn establishes four basic elements of pragmatic religious naturalism: (1) a push beyond supernaturalism; (2) religion as a human construction; (3) religion as a synergy of "the real and the ideal" [40]; and (4) hope guided by realities of embodied life. In the case of Du Bois this is filtered through the realities of race and racism within the United States—the push and pull against black bodies within private worlds and public arenas. His form of religious naturalism could not avoid the promise and pitfalls of black life in the United States, and the haunting chronicle of that life found in the signs and symbols of faith within African American communities. In light of this contextual shift Du Bois's religious naturalism can be said to encapsulate five primary moves reminiscent of the four points above: (1) no interest in metaphysics and supernaturalism; (2) religion provides a language for tackling the sociopolitical and economic concerns of mundane life; (3) religion provides a way of maintaining creative tension between African Americans as part of the larger fabric of American collective life and African Americans as a distinct group; (4) the framing of this religiosity is dependent on mechanisms of thought and action—"piety, Jeremiadic protest, and sacrifice;" and finally, (5) the first four encourage an understanding of Du Bois's religious identity as defined by a process of seeking meaning through destruction of the traditional linkages of sociopolitical, economic, and religious claims in and on the United States. With religion so conceived, activism against racism is a spiritual action. It is a spiritual practice to the extent the term spiritual has nothing to do with cosmic and supernatural forces but instead concerns attention on human finitude and the challenges of life lodged within that historical arrangement.

Old ways of being religious and doing religion are problematic for Du Bois. They push against recognition of the "everyday" and urge speculation concerning something beyond what the senses can discern and reason can interrogate. He provides cautionary tales of religion blinding people to their needs and opportunities, and thereby distracting them from the real work at hand. For Blum, religious commitment demands a tackling of human life—an effort to transform it for the better—as the social import of the faith. Du Bois, as Kahn also presents him, holds to a religious orientation that demands human action within human arenas because it is all we have. There is no looking up to the heavens for some type of assistance but rather we must be content to look to humans for whatever creativity and activity we can muster.

Religion operates with a keen awareness of the tragic nature of life—the shortcomings, abuses, traumas, and pains that mark out human existence. For Christianity, problems result in theological turmoil—for example, theodicy—but for Du Bois problems are not so destabilizing. They are the givens of human life and finitude that are to be wrestled strategically and systematically in the pursuit of something better. He renders the very struggle for life and life meaning a religious quest solidly and firmly lodged in the arena of embodied, historical, and communal existence keenly sensitive to the ways in which black bodies occupy time and space. It is political and informed by the experiences that mark out black life in the United States. That attention to remembering—as a matter of piety—acknowledges and honors African American ancestors as central to the structuring of the United States. There is a dualism of intent at work as well in that this remembering captures the Jeremiad found within African American culture by means of which African Americans critique current sociopolitical and economic arrangements while offering a democratic and affirming alternative.

Albeit different on so many levels, both Kahn and Blum are fixed on the idea that Du Bois represents a break with former ways of thinking and doing religion—a break with African American (and American) religion as played out prior to his emergence as a major voice. He is not simply mimicking Enlightenment claims, nor is he reducing religion to morality. It is for Du Bois more than this because, as Kahn notes, "it provides the political bravery and the courage to seek the greater moral good; it provides the good with its vigor, its captivating qualities, and its ability to ensoul, which is to say to sustain people through tragedy and suffering." (6) As Blum needed a sense of religion that could absorb the critical thinking of Du Bois who denounces certain framings and naming of the religious, Kahn needs a sense of religion that can maintain its integrity by absorbing even what appears a rejection of religion. In this way, Du Bois can be presented as stepping away from a religion that damages reason and activism because it safeguards magic and irrational claims. Religion for Kahn's Du Bois is grounded in the mundane, wedded to embodied existence and all its demands and shortcomings. And religious language functions as a poetics of life meant to do damage to injustices that restrict the nature and meaning of life. It is this use of religion that Kahn believes is captured by Du Bois's phrase "divine discontent" used to name religious images and ideals that capture the issues of his times. Although this is not as clearly the case with Blum, there is here nothing *sui generis* about religion, but rather Du Bois's religion is religious because it captures some of what we have meant by religion (although it dismisses some of what has been labeled as religion).

The Jeremiad, as Du Bois provides it in texts such as *Souls of Black Folk*, envisions a democratic arrangement challenging ideological structures and practices. It is not a code for inclusion in the existing frameworks of life in the United States but rather it demands reconstruction of life so as to recognize and incorporate as vital and vibrant the experiences of African Americans. Yet, it is a call for a certain type of symmetry whereby African Americans as a distinct community (i.e., a nation of sorts) exists with integrity as part of the larger framing of the United States. This new type of life is for Du Bois the equivalent of salvation achieved through a spiritual practice of sacrifice (i.e., dedicated work toward the improvement of life within the confines of history). For Kahn, and in a certain way for Blum, this is how one should understand the transfigurations of Christ through which African American experience of violent discrimination speaks to the larger reshaping of collective life. These black Christ figures are not suffering servants or sacrificial beings in a traditional sense because nothing is taken from them and they are not establishing a model of conduct to be emulated. Rather, they are agents of transformation whose self-determined activities urge recognition of the integrity and significance of African American embodied life. These figures confront the stultifying effects of undemocratic ideological formulations and practices.

Replete with Christian signs and symbols, use of religious language in presenting these Christ-like figures points to the religious baring witness to the presence of their own. In a word, the religious recognize in Du Bois's description of these figures something organic, representative, and compelling. This is not to say Du Bois and the masses of African American Christians held to the same basic theological structuring, nor is it to say that his religious orientation was without complications and tensions. "If in breaths Du Bois sounded deeply irreligious depths, expressing for example genuine doubt about the existence of God," Kahn writes, "in other breaths, indeed, at times in the next breath, he expressed deep devotional desires." (5) Nonetheless, his writings serve as a litmus test, a linguistic trail, that Kahn believes can give a sense of Du Bois's personal take on religion. This requires that one carefully follow the trail and do so without an uncritical irreligious bias and assumption. The book is Kahn's recounting of this process of discovery and analysis—marking out a trail highlighting something of the faith that captures Du Bois and how it is expressed in his life and writings.

The moral thinker's religion

Kahn and Blum argue their books are not concerned primarily with establishing Du Bois as religious in any particular way, although they are quick to point out he was not an atheist but rather was religious (theistic?) in a particular way. It is only in light of this religious self—or a particular cipher—they are then able to outline how religion functions within his writings. In this way, his personal faith stance—described in competing ways—stands as a hermeneutic by means of which to explore the nature and import of religion in his various types of public writing. Johnson's project is a bit different, although he also sees investigation of Du Bois's take on religion as a way of maneuvering with meaning and purpose through the tangles of contemporary life.[6] Blum and Kahn are concerned with the promotion of a new vocabulary, a new grammar of life, made possible through the theistic language of black existence captured in Du Bois' writings. This concern is no less present in Johnson's book. For all three, proper discourse shapes proper action in a sense, and religion continues to have a role in this—when applied to contemporary circumstances by religious people.

Thinking of Du Bois as a prophet, or a kind of "moral priest," Johnson speaks of Du Bois's "moral imagination" (alternately labeled ethical imagination) as being of more importance than efforts to discern his personal religious orientation. This is because moral imagination "speaks to the framework he developed in his search for alternative ways of imagining freedom and justice in a society that, during his lifetime, rendered blacks invisible or inferior." (11) Furthermore, he is a prophet, as Johnson understands him, not because of commitment to a particular theistic orientation, but because of special insights he shares with others.

Like Kahn, Johnson is keen to understand religion not as *sui generis*, but rather it is a tool by means of which to decipher life, and as such no particular theological claims are necessary. However, unlike Kahn, Johnson wants to resist (although this is short-lived) assuming this use of religion comes from a particularly religious man—naturalistic or not. For Johnson it is sufficient to say he is an exemplar of moral insight and action. Where Blum and Kahn see religious commitment, Johnson observes moral thought. While not addressing Kahn directly on this score, he does challenge Blum's claim that Du Bois is a Christian and an early framer of liberation theology. Johnson wants the reader to believe neither is an important or necessary claim in order to capture the moral wisdom offered in Du Bois's corpus. Reflecting on John Rawls and Du Bois, Johnson acknowledges agreed-on religious practices and beliefs are not possible or necessary. Instead, attention must be given to agreement regarding the language and dynamics of egalitarian life. Where Du Bois corrects Rawls is on the plain of racism, on blackness as a moral problem that impacts conversation concerning and activism toward justice and democratic living. That is to say, Du Bois exposes the tragic dimensions of life that others ignore, and he does so by exposing racism as affecting every dimension of human be*ing*.

Is Du Bois able to maintain a healthy tension in line with Johnson's claims, whereby he recognizes religious diversity as a good thing, through his use of signs and symbols from a variety of religious possibilities, including what Johnson labels "Afro-Christianity, African religions, and Western moral traditions . . ."? (111) Johnson leans in the direction of a "yes," but, like the other authors, he is unable to hold a creative tension and quickly moves to understand Du Bois as motivated by the haunting beauty of black Christianity and its vision of life. This is most telling when Johnson says, "I agree with Manning Marable's assessment of Du Bois's religious commitments: he was a 'staunch critic of religious dogma' and a passionate convert to the black version of Christianity." (112) Here Du Bois's religion is a form shifting model, but one most easily expressed as a modality of Christian faith—but an old faith, borne of the ancestors as opposed to a twentieth-century version. It is an old faith that might just tell the careful observer something about the nature of race and racism—or life behind the "Veil." By describing the "Veil," Du Bois, from Johnson's perspective, pushes public discourse beyond its comfort zone, beyond the limits of an abstract and disembodied political liberalism. This is a transformative process with moral implications in that it fights racism and repositions African Americans as fully human, as persons of worth and value.

Du Bois's earthy, material religion and politics form a synergistic relationship that is best described as moral thinking from an "ethical guide." (11) He is this guide because he understands the nature of the "Veil" and the workings of US life, and has a word of transformation deciphered from the cultural output of the people and in line with a robust moral vision. There is nothing metaphysical or supernatural about this moral vision; rather it is no more than an illuminating take on the value of and work toward renewed existence. Du Bois, according to Johnson, offers a way of naming and categorizing the experience of African American ancestors—the souls of black folk—as a mode of "tragic soul-life." Kahn briefly notes this category, but of the three only Johnson sees it as a hermeneutic and moral framing of life robust and deep enough to harness and guide struggle toward democracy. For him tragic soul-life entails an intriguing process of pushing beyond simple political life to the full flourishing of subjective freedom marked by reflexive agency. It is the demise of the self, understood only in stultifying racialized terms, and the emergence of an embodied being self-conscious and aware. In other words, "tragic soul-life," writes Johnson, "is the beauty that surfaces when death and despair are confronted by unyielding hope in divine and political justice" and in this way it maps internal stirrings filled with longing and resolve. It is through attention to the workings of tragic soul-life that one gets a sense of what undergirds Du Bois moral thinking and his praxis (38–9).

It, tragic soul-life, holds in creative tension and explains something about religion and sociopolitical existence and in this way it can support a penetrating discourse on public life. This is the case because it speaks most forcefully to the meaning of what Du Bois called "the problem of the color line," and it plays into both moral failures and the possibility of democracy. The concept tragic soul-life is key to transformed living, but it is a concept whose application demands numerous steps. First, it requires rethinking the self in a way that points to a robust discussion of how the individual and the group are formulated, particularly in light of double consciousness. This must be followed by a push beyond racialized notions of the self that restrict value and worth. Finally, application of tragic soul-life necessitates the introduction of two concepts—"soul" and "soul-beauty" as markers of self and self-worth that have the capacity to reshape public conversation around once despised populations. It is important to note distinctions in this use of soul in *Tragic Soul-Life*. Here it is a conceptual device whereas for Blum it has something to do with what progressive Christianity understands as the innermost (somewhat metaphysical) element of our being. In this regard, the soul noted above in relationship to Johnson's framing is the "genius," or the dynamics of an internal life and vantage point that is able to resist racism and project out through the embodied being a new vision even in the midst of despair (44).

This work of resistance can involve death, and for Johnson death is never far from Du Bois thoughts. Death—the demise of a bound and fixed racial self—is always found in relationship to struggle for "subjective freedom" as a sphere of possibility. And, it constitutes demise graphically depicted in the transfigurations of Christ offered by Du Bois through lynched bodies. As is the case with Kahn, Johnson believes these stories of new Christ figures are not a call for a traditional theologizing of the Christ Event read through twentieth-century racial politics. These stories—like Du Bois's nonfiction writings—speak to the necessity (and possibility) of hope even within a sphere of demise. More recent work such as Toni Morrison's *Beloved* becomes a testament to the nature of death and hope that inform and shape Du Bois's sense of tragic soul-life. *Beloved*, like Du Bois's writings, speaks to an embodied confrontation with history and death, but with the ever-present desire for more. As Morrison demonstrates and Du Bois hopes, something can emerge on the other side of death in the form of a deep "beauty," a type of resolve and persistence for life expressed within the genius of African Americans. When thinking of freedom related to this process, Johnson finds in Frederick Douglass an example entailing more than greater space for political engagement, but instead he notes Douglass's attention to the new person working within troubled contexts lacking proper moral imagination. The take away: despair and hope are both important, if the ethical challenges facing the United States are to be noted and addressed thoughtfully and productively.

As Johnson reads Du Bois, "a soul-oriented conception of the self" is a prime way of naming the being of this new person who is more than her existential circumstances proscribed by a warped social imagination. A need to seriously wrestle with, reflect on, and remember the nastiness of the US past and present informs what both Kahn and Johnson understand as the touchstone of transformation. It is only through this turn to the past—its actors and activities—forms of healthy identity are possible and the potential for democratic living realized.

Tragic Soul-Life is intended to uncover the manner in which racism in the United States rest on a bed of religious, political, and moral failure which Du Bois points out with power and through a poetic turn to the tragic as a moral compass. "By turning to tragic soul-life," Johnson argues, "we discover a point that Du Bois spent his life developing: that the underlying principles of democracy ought to protect and promote human aspirations that reflect ideal (what should be) and historic specific circumstances." (6) Again, tragic soul-life is able to accomplish so much, to have such centrality, because it recognizes the roles played by politics and religion in the construction of a racist society, and only attention to both through profound moral thinking can undo these circumstances. This is the case because injustice should be understood as "spiritual isolation" which entails an embodied moral crisis premised on bad moral assumptions. This isolation, a type of deep damage, is expressed in the religious yearnings and frustrations in the spirituals, or what Du Bois described as the sorrow songs. These songs, like spiritual isolation, represent both a lament of suffering and the means by which to resolve the sufferings caused by racism. In essence, like Blum and Kahn, Johnson argues the cultural worlds constructed by African Americans and expressed through religious imagery and language inform and fuel Du Bois's writings and activism. His use of religion and religious language shapes a moral discourse. This is for Du Bois, Johnson wants readers to understand, the way to shape ethics as a proper venue by means of which to transform the politics of life.

Johnson's book aims to read public life in the United States through religious and political conversation (best understood as a type of synergistic relationship)—filtered through Du Bois' concept of tragic soul-life and his notion of race as the twentieth-century problem. The end result is Johnson's take on renewed conversation concerning and action toward transformed public life that pushes us to risk new territories of possibility beyond where we have felt most at ease.

Read together, these three books share a conviction that the various genres of his writing speak in powerful ways to the realities of life in the twentieth century in part because of their use of religious language to shape perceptions of suffering and progress. Yet, how to read Du Bois's personal commitments remains a challenge, and while this question of personal faith stance is important for all three authors need it be? Can only "insiders" properly understand and appreciate the religious worlds and the language used to explore them? These authors seem to suggest the answer is "yes," a qualified "yes," but a "yes" nonetheless. Still, the differences of opinion between these three authors point to the difficulty of such claims, while their thoughtful texts highlight the continued significance of his writings. With no unquestionable argument on the topic in place, perhaps we must be comfortable with the idea that Du Bois's thinking on and use of religion is complex, layered, thick, as well as full of tensions and paradox. Ultimately, Du Bois's continuing importance rest not on his personal religious beliefs—whatever form they did or did not take—but on the sharpness of his insights and his profound ability to unpack and interrogate the inner workings of racialized life in the United States.

And so . . .

Du Bois's thinking on and use of religion is complex, layered, thick, as well as full of tensions and paradox. If one looks for a traditional theological orientation in Du Bois, frustration results: this type of religious understanding is lost in Du Bois.[7] Sometime after his graduate training, Du Bois would frame his basic sense of metaphysics in this way: "I do not believe in the existence and rulership of the one God of the Jews. I do not believe in the miraculous birth and the miracles of the Christ of the Christians; I do not believe in many of the tenets of Mohammedanism [sic] and Buddhism; and frankly I do not believe that the Guardian of the Bahai' faith has any supernatural knowledge."[8] His religious sensibilities are not in line with dominant and institutional modalities of religious encounter and worship. Yet, Du Bois is not without a religious and theological side expressed through an appreciation for the cultural significance of certain signs and symbols, but it is one I would describe as naturalistic humanism, or what others refer to as "skeptical agnosticism," or "religious naturalism."[9] (He even references the readers of *The Souls of Black Folk* as "O God the Reader." [*Souls*, 191])

Tied to this stance was his commitment to sociology, and hence, he was not opposed to exploring, learning something about, and writing about the faith of African Americans. A mistake is made, however, when readers assume this sociological presentation of religion involves a personal embrace of theistic doctrine, creeds, and practices. It all looked like "narrow dogma" (*Dusk*, 57) to Du Bois, and for that he had no use.

He speaks of the religious worlds of African Americans, shaped in part through a sense of the spiritual as conceptual paradigm or, better yet, hermeneutic. But, he does so with some distance and by means of an agnostic stance (e.g., deep distrust of dogma's ability to deaden a reasonable posture toward the world). Du Bois makes use of religious grammar and vocabulary but he does so in a manner that strips both of any metaphysical significance. They are merely tools useful in unpacking what appears to be a less than compelling cultural discourse and practice—theism.[10]

Theological grammar and vocabulary become ways to connote elements of our existence—ontological meaning, emotions, and so on—that are not responsive to his more scientific inclinations. This grammar and vocabulary are put to a different service and appear to lack connection to transcendental markers of super-historical situated arrangements. Rather even in more vague presentation, these markers of a religious language speak to the historical arrangements of collective life. Take for example, his presentation of suffrage. "Thus Negro suffrage ended a civil war by beginning a race feud," he writes, and continues, "and some felt gratitude toward the race thus sacrificed in its swaddling clothes on the altar of national integrity" (*Souls*, 33). A reference to the birth of Jesus the Christ as the source of redemption and, by extension, an illusion to a transfiguration of Christ in the form of sacrificed African Americans, Du Bois renders redemption political while the spiritual announces it as theological: "Children, go where I send Thee; How will I send Thee, I'm a-going to send Thee One by one as was the little baby born, born in Bethlehem."[11]

Perhaps there is something in African Americans as a group in "swaddling clothes on the altar of national integrity," that is like Josie—the young girl he meets as a Fisk University student seeking a summer teaching assignment. Like Josie, perhaps African Americans have "a certain fineness, the shadow of an unconscious moral heroism that would willingly give all of life to make life broader, deeper, and fuller for her and hers." (*Souls*, 50) Even when discussing the spirituals, or what he calls the sorrow songs, despite their rich theological formulations, he sets his sights on a more mundane dimension of their meaning:

> Through all the sorrow of the Sorrow Songs there breathes a hope—a faith in the ultimate justice of things. The minor cadences of despair change often to triumph and calm confidence. Sometimes it is faith in life, sometimes a faith in death, sometimes assurance of boundless justice in some fair world beyond. But whichever it is, the meaning is always clear: that sometime, somewhere, men will judge men by their souls and not by their skins. (*Souls*, 188)

The grammar and vocabulary—in this instance of sacrifice and redemption—lend themself to mapping out to a certain degree the workings of the human soul. They map the content and form of expression—the articulation of the genius or ideals of the people—that are not fully captured through scientific formulas. African American faith as he sees and appreciates it involves a strong commitment to principles of liberty and democracy, to the substance of the person beyond what dollars and political maneuvers are meant to detect. And, this commitment, this framing of faith, makes for Du Bois so much of the parsing of religiosity irrelevant.

Du Bois, near the end of *The Souls of Black Folk*, tells the story of a young African American—John Jones—who is sent away to school and returns to his little town with new ideas that startle the people. And, maybe, there is something of Du Bois in John's statement one evening in church; perhaps it speaks to Du Bois's approach to religion in general and theism in particular. "To-day," John remarks, "the world cares little whether a man be Baptist or Methodist, or indeed a churchman at all, so long as he is good and true. What difference does it make whether a man be baptized in river or wash-bowl, or not at all? Let's leave all that littleness, and look higher." (*Souls*, 174)

SECTION TWO

Religion

Whether one embraces it or not, religion has played a significant role in the shaping of human encounters with/in the world. Religious sensibilities and principles have enhanced human life, but just as often they have dimensioned the dignity and health of life (of which humans are only a component). Humanists and other nontheists, unlike with the issue of race, have been very vocal—typically offering ways to reject and move beyond religion. Some have gone so far as to argue religion is the source of all human tragedy. While there are problems with religious outlooks, is aggressive antagonism the best approach? And, on a more basic level, do humanists and atheists have a useful understanding of religion and religious experience?

In the chapters for this section I offer an alternate understanding of religion, one that seeks to distinguish religion from theism. I argue theism is the issue that must be addressed, whereas religion is simply a structuring of human experience meant to help humans find life's meaning. Nontheists and theists both seek to make life meaningful. Chapters in this section also provide an alternate way of thinking about the Bible so as to allow humanists to find some meaning in the text. This is done through a study of Nimrod as cultural hero over against the biblical God as a mode of discourse meant to limit human creativity, ingenuity, and community. The idea of Jesus the Christ is similarly deconstructed. Although critical of certain dimensions of theism (as a mode of religion), this section also points out something done rather well by theists: the formation of communities for ritualization of important life developments. Humanists, nontheists in general, are giving increased attention to community; and in the final chapter of this section I discuss two examples of this quest for the humanist ritualization of ordinary life in community.

5

Nimrod is a hero... and God is a problem

This first chapter involves a shift, a movement away from naming humanism as it relates to issues of race to a discussion of the use of humanism as a way to understand and, when necessary, dismantle traditional modalities of theism. Mindful of this goal, what better place to begin then with the conceptual framework holding theism together: God?

Humanism, the form privileged by this book, has been quick to denounce the idea of God as a harmful conceptual category—over against science—that allows for and supports human wrongs such as racism and other modalities of dehumanization.[1] And while so much of this argument is true, it is typically built on assumptions regarding the Bible that are similar to the assumptions made by theists. That is to say, humanists and Bible believers tend to both argue from the premise that the Bible says something worth arguing over. For believers (e.g., Christians) it says something of value about the morals and ethics necessary to live a productive and happy life, and for the humanist there is also the assumption it says something about how to live and this "something" must be countered by reason and logic. I agree with much of this latter perspective; yet, I think it should entail not a dismissal of the Bible but an interrogation of the scriptures through a humanist lens. The Bible contains the seeds of its own irrelevance, but also noteworthy ideals of substantial significance for a humanist life orientation. A prime example of what I have in mind is the story of Nimrod, used to support racial discrimination and the authority of God, but also offering a celebration of human dignity and ingenuity.

> Cush was the father of Nimrod, who became a mighty warrior on the earth. He was a mighty hunter before the Lord; that is why it is said, "Like Nimrod, a mighty hunter before the Lord." The first centers of his kingdom were Babylon, Uruk, Akkad and Kalneh, in Shinar. From that land he went to Assyria, where he built Nineveh, Rehoboth Ir, Calah and Resen, which is between Nineveh and Calah—which is the great city. (Gen. 10:8-12)

Tackling this story gives humanists an opportunity to tackle two problems—race-based discrimination and God—and also develop an icon of humanist existence of the same merit as Sisyphus or Prometheus. Sisyphus has his rock as punishment from Zeus; Prometheus his ravenous bird picking daily his liver as punishment from Zeus; and Nimrod his tower destroyed by an angry God of the Hebrews. All three, within different contexts, speak to a similar anthropological perspective that should be of deep interest to humanists. Two versions of this anthropology told from within the context of Greece, and the third—Nimrod—spoken about a descendant of Ham discussed in Genesis 9, of Africa.

Why have not humanists given more attention to rethinking biblical figures such as Nimrod, who has been used unduly as a marker of divinely sanctioned discrimination? Must traditional and dehumanizing interpretations of such figures stand unchallenged? In this chapter, I answer this question with a strong "no," and I offer evidence for this through an interpretation of Nimrod and the Tower of Babel made possible through a hermeneutic centered on human creativity and the value of risk.

> Now the whole world had one language and a common speech. As people moved eastward, they found a plain in Shinarand settled there. They said to each other, "Come, let's make bricks and bake them thoroughly." They used brick instead of stone, and tar for mortar. Then they said, "Come, let us build ourselves a city, with a tower that reaches to the heavens, so that we may make a name for ourselves; otherwise we will be scattered over the face of the whole earth." But the Lord came down to see the city and the tower the people were building. The Lord said, "If as one people speaking the same language they have begun to do this, then nothing they plan to do will be impossible for them. Come, let us go down and confuse their language so they will not understand each other." So the Lord scattered them from there over all the earth, and they stopped building the city. That is why it was called Babel—because there the Lord confused the language of the whole world. From there the Lord scattered them over the face of the whole earth. (Gen. 11:1-9)

My purpose in applying humanism to this scriptural story of Nimrod is to provide alternate readings of "sacred" stories in ways that promote human welfare.

That is to say, some have Prometheus, who is celebrated for giving a gift to humanity and suffering great, perpetual pain as a consequence; and, others have Sisyphus, who is punished by having to roll a great stone up a hill only to have it roll down and the process start again. They, as Albert Camus would note, are "Absurd Heroes," whose actions accomplish no end product and for whom there is no resolution. I argue Nimrod falls into this category; indeed, he is the greatest of "Absurd Heroes" in that he does not simply trick gods (as does Sisyphus) or steal from gods (as does Prometheus). No, he causes God to fear a human, to be troubled by human capacity and its potentiality.

He, Nimrod, creates something that threatens the place of the Grand Unity of the Universe known as God—or, what we might reference as limit, that is, humanity's *modus agendi*. He unites people around their creativity and capacity "to do," and he structures this mutuality in profound ways with felt consequences that speak to the synergistic relationship between success and failure.

This is the greater thing: Nimrod achieves nothing—other than infamy through the pen of church leaders such as St Augustine. The Force (i.e., God) given credit for humanity's creativity and ingenuity destroys the most compelling sign of that creativity. Humans who were to seek closeness to God are punished—divided and isolated from each other—for seeking both spiritual and physical proximity to God. In a word, humans, as far as the story suggests, are punished for seeking the closeness lost when forced out the Garden of Eden and for which they are predisposed to long. Isn't there something absurd about this? Humans called to God, desired closeness to God and God's world—and this great hunter and leader, Nimrod, means to provide a mechanism for achieving it. He seeks to use the stuff of material existence to achieve a particular metaphysical connection to that which is beyond this materiality. As such, he is a proper iconic figure, a fitting symbol, and conceptual paradigm capable of undergirding and carrying humanism and humanists forward.

My first efforts to work through the humanist significance of Nimrod were made as a way of framing the epistemological and ethical structuring of African American humanism. But, Nimrod's importance extends beyond just that one community of humanists. I would argue this is particularly compelling—a shift from Sisyphus and Prometheus to Nimrod—as humanist organizations and atheist organizations struggle with diversity and a positive assessment and ethics of difference.

Thinking about Nimrod

Christian discussions of despised figures—for example, Ham, Canaan, Nimrod—have implied softened versions of the traditional legends. Yet, as I have noted for some time now, a humanist read allows for new possibilities, ones that promote "a reconstitution of a forgotten tradition of human integrity, a type of 'subjugated knowledge,'" suggesting as it does, "the possibility of nurturing creativity and potential in transforming ways."[2] Although he is typically discussed as a theological problem, a descendant of Ham, and as one whose efforts damaged the relationship between God and humanity resulting in the dispersal of humanity and the confusion of language, I argue that his actions celebrate human ingenuity and creativity. Nimrod unifies a community around a common objective, a common goal—whereas God's activities in this story are questionably insecure at best and demonic (in the sense of life destroying life) at worse.

Religious life and thought have been dominated by assumptions concerning the proper posture toward the Universe (or God), premised in part on subtle reference to the "crime" of human self-importance and growth chronicled in the Book of Genesis: the Garden of Eden, the alleged curse on Canaan, and the story of Nimrod. God set up self-assertion in the Garden of Eden as the problem that must be punished, the impetus for actions that should not be taken. And this action in the case of the former, the Garden of Eden, serves as the theo-ethical rationale, a form of determinism, for the stories of Canaan and Nimrod. The following scriptural passages provide a sense of this problematizing of human action:

And the Lord God said, Behold the man is become as one of us, to know good and evil: and now, lest he put forth his hand, and take also of the tree of life, and eat, and live for ever; therefore the Lord God sent him forth from the garden of Eden, to till the ground from whence he was taken. So he drove out the man . . .[3]

And he [Noah] said, Cursed be Canaan; a servant of servants shall he be unto his brethren.[4]

And they said, Go to, let us build us a city and a Tower, whose top may reach unto heaven: and let us make us a name, lest we be scattered abroad upon the face of the whole earth. And the Lord came down to see the city and the tower, which the children of men builded. And the Lord said, Behold, the people is one, and they have all one language; and this they begin to do: and now nothing will be restrained from them, which they have imagined to do.[5]

In all three of the above episodes, the relayed behavior of the divine is premised on a felt impingement on a freedom that threatens the epistemological and ontological distinction between divine and human that the concept of God is meant to safeguard. Addressing this involves at least two possibilities:

1 A reformulation of the God idea in ways that provide space for a positive autonomy as the mark of humanity; and
2 A negative conception of humanity that renders problematic the exercise of autonomy or independence.

The second is chosen. Hence, tied to the above stories is a negative theological anthropology, one that renders problematic human ingenuity. There, however, is an alternate reading of Nimrod, one premised on humanist sensibilities.

God as restraint exposed

This story is not solely about Nimrod—about the movements of humans in time and space. Rather it is an indictment of a particularly restrictive metaphysics—a placing of that metaphysics on trial, within the courtroom of human self-realization. This story of Nimrod tells a great deal about the conception of God.

For the sake of argument, I am not interested in whether or not there is a "being," some type of trans/historical "reality," we rightly call God; rather, my focus is on the impact of this concept, the language of God regardless of whether or not this concept points to a substantive cosmic presence. Whether "real" or "mythic" this conception of God, as a matter of language, focuses attention, defines epistemological and ethical boundaries, and shapes life. Again, it serves as the structuring of *modus agendi*. It is this function that I am interested in exploring through a humanist theological interpretation of Nimrod that privileges creativity and the value of risk.

The ramifications of this alternate read are significant in that, for example, the Genesis discussion of human free will might entail an act of bad faith, a deception on the part of the discourse of/on God. There is a battle between the logic and workings of the conception of God and the human desire for fullness of being. God serves to stifle this push for a greater sense of being.[6] Again I point to divine anxiety:

> And the Lord God said, Behold the man is become as one of us, to know good and evil: and now, lest he put forth his hand, and take also of the tree of life, and eat, and live for ever; therefore the Lord God sent him forth from the garden of Eden, to till the ground from whence he was taken. So he drove out the man . . .[7]

The rest of salvation history—the story of God's effort to connect with humanity—involves an effort to maintain this bad faith and its connotation. Here I suggest that God is the metasymbol of restraint: Restraint is God; God is the logic of *modus agendi*.[8] Some might argue the Nimrod account promotes the proper and favorable view of God entailing divinity as a necessary restriction on human activity. If nothing else, others might suggest, it points to the very nature of religious devotion. What Frank Brown says in his discussion of the relationship between aesthetics and religion bears on this notion of Restraint as foundational within religion. He says: "As has often been observed, whatever is religious naturally 'serves as an agent of closure', shutting off human investigation, criticism, and effort in deference to the authority of the more-than-human, the supernatural, the other-worldly."[9] Christians have traditionally understood this limitation on human creativity and imagination as a fundamental good—a way of protecting us from ourselves. But is this a necessary, or even the most appropriate, theological interpretation of Restraint?

It appears to me that the concept of Restraint as God does not exercise this type of authority for the good of humanity. Nimrod's move strikes me as a wrestling against the assumption of inevitable wrongness, misdeed, due to an assumed original sin that blueprints humans for improper activity if left to their own devices. It is a strike against an external force that controls human destiny, and the establishment of human ingenuity and creativity in its place.

Human creativity in community

Through a traditional reading of the text, we are to believe that Nimrod's action is an attempt to be God—to assume the shape and posture of the biblical God—and to promote a form of imperialism. Yet a humanist read (influenced by existentialism viewed through the lens of humanist theology) does not revolve around an assumed effort on the part of Nimrod to assert his will as "God" over against those around him—to live without regard to the welfare of others. Nimrod does not view himself as alone in the world, one whose will and freedom demand the negation of others.

The angst belongs to Restraint as God, not Nimrod: Human creativity requires destruction, and in this case the destruction involves a blow against Restraint as God's supremacy—its ability to define the perimeters of human movement. One can argue that, through the building of the Tower, Nimrod rebels against a certain type of metaphysically imposed limitation on human creativity and action. Restraint as God had been the source of fear, beginning with Adam and Eve's encounter with God in the Garden, and dread in that the pervasiveness of Restraint as God meant humanity could not escape a sense of burden, of something pressing on them, restricting them, overdetermining them, owning them. Nimrod rebels, not through words but through the exercise of will with and on behalf of others.

Nimrod's rebellion is not a radical freedom, the type that supports amorality; it cares about the individual but that individual within the context of relationships. Nimrod, based on the implications of the construction of the Tower, is mindful of the consequences of his actions for community. His is not best described as a *freedom* **from**, but a *freedom* **to**—a freedom *to* develop meaning within the context of community. It is a freedom in responsibility as opposed to a freedom from responsibility.

Nimrod's actions suggest a sense of interdependence, of mutuality—but one that allows humans to build their world, however compromised and fragile those structures may be. But this posture works against Restraint as God. Isn't it for this reason that the dispersal—the confusing of language takes place, according to the story?

The creation account in Genesis points to the power of language because God is said to speak things into existence. By destroying a unified language (i.e., discourse as a creative device): Restraint as God seeks to accomplish the demise of human creativity as a communal endeavor. Restraint as God, not human freedom, imposes isolation, loneliness. The following is God's response to Nimrod's project:

> And the Lord said, Behold, the people is one, and they have all one language; and this they begin to do; and now nothing will be restrained from them, which they have imagined to do. Go to, let us go down, and there confound their language, that they may not understand one another's speech. So the Lord scattered them abroad from thence upon the face of the earth . . .[10]

Nimrod's exercise of human ingenuity and creativity is projected as an offense, but it is only an offense against the status quo, against Restraint as God. Restraint as God is concerned with the unified assertion of collective will—the effort of humans to expand themselves within the context of community, and in this way achieve what one alone cannot.

God's great fear

Restraint as God is able to address self-will because it can be approached through force, by means of a power that limits the individual. Hence, self-will poses no hard threat to divine integrity. However, this community-based act of freedom that moves beyond self-will is more difficult for Restraint as God in that it poses a threat to the very need for the divine as a unifying principle.

Human maturation, as presented by Nimrod, entails the absorption of restraint, the recognition that restraint must issue from the inner self, and be promoted by and for the self in relationship to community, and that it does not rightly issue from some external force. It is an act of bad faith—the belief that determinations should be surrendered to some external force. The story of Restraint as God has involved an attempt to cover this through acts of aggression and denouncement, talk of a divine and overarching will positioned to control human interactions. Nimrod epistemologically and existentially breaks this open. Damage is done to the metaphysical groundings of Restraint.

Existentially and epistemologically speaking, Restraint as God imposes limits on humanity—freedom and responsibility inscribed in a world that is monitored ultimately by divinely imposed parameters of life. Yet, Nimrod's activities entail the saturation of life, of human *being*, with freedom, responsibility, and accountability in a world in which human creativity and ingenuity trump the divine.

With Nimrod's action a new epistemology is introduced, one that does not recognize Restraint as God as necessary: God is not the ultimate response to the question of meaning, the question of being, and the question of existence. The Tower symbolizes the effort to make meaning, to confront existence. Nimrod does not deny the existence of God, rather the Tower demonstrates an effort, as critics have rightly noted but not appreciated, to replace God with human possibility, and to address the consequences of that replacement—the effort to create a new paradigm of human existence. Perhaps the destruction of the Tower and the spreading of humanity point not only to the ultimate accountability of humans for their life, but also to the brittle and fragile nature of the outcomes of this accountability when exercised.

Nimrod's efforts, although ultimately resulting in failure, point out the illusionary nature of Restraint as God's control over humans.

Free will has caught God—and Nimrod points to the scope of this freedom that God seeks to limit. Nimrod's action points to the act of bad faith perpetrated by Restraint as God in the Garden of Eden: Restraint as God does not want true fellowship. The possibility that those in fellowship will think differently, will challenge, and perhaps threaten the cosmic structure, the theologically contrived status quo—"They will become as us . . . "—creates discord with Restraint as God.

This conceptualization of God was never the same after the events in the first eleven chapters of Genesis. First beginning to lose its grip on humanity in the Garden of Eden, Nimrod compromises it further, raising a question of ontological and epistemological import: Is it possible to live without Restraint as God, without an externally erected sense of communal responsibility and cooperation?

Learning from Nimrod

Nimrod encourages humans to be themselves, to live with consequences—pleasant and unpleasant though they may be. Nimrod offers replacement of Restraint as God with human creativity and ingenuity. But this is not a vulgar appeal to human freedom that means do as you please. Rather, as the building of the Tower suggests, this freedom, this dethroning of restraint in cosmic grab involves a responsibility for productive movement—for a fellowship of sorts that takes into consideration the "whole" when acting.

Radical individualism poses no deep threat to God as restraint in that effort to be alone ultimately brings into focus the utility of this particular God idea. However, Nimrod's is a different narrative, a more troubling possibility from the perspective of Restraint as God: Nimrod's freedom is intermingled with attention to others. Such a freedom destroys the integrity of Restraint as God rather than pointing to a defect in humanity. And it does so by questioning metaphysically imposed limitations on human development, and by an implied critique of determinism generated by a theology of original sin. Nimrod exposes the nature of Restraint as God: a fragile and unnecessary concept.

Nimrod's act is the first significant act of human creation. Adam and Eve name what Restraint as God is said to have created—but this is not the same, although the application of language is a certain type of creation. Yet the building of the Tower is another, one that does not confirm the idea of Restraint as God, but rather brings it into question—punching holes in its supremacy.

Ultimately the Tower fails not because it represents an unreasonable assertion of human will, one that must be checked through divine intervention. No, Nimrod's action does damage to Restraint as God that prevents it from having the authority over human will that it once enjoyed. Rather, it fails, I argue, because Nimrod's exercise of human will involves the tragic, a push for human betterment that celebrates achievement while recognizing its shortcomings. The Tower, as an act of will, contains both a promise and a pitfall: it reflects human creativity and human limitation. (This is something humanists would do well to remember.) Its construction is a morally and ethically responsible act of will, yet this expression of will does not get humans all that is desired. Will and creativity are what humans have, but they accomplish only so much. Nonetheless, it is not a problem that Nimrod's project fails. Instead, this failure is simply recognition through metaphor that humans are prone to difficulties—moments of collapse—often culminating in some sort of demise, in this case the demise of a dream.

The Tower project comes to an end, but what could not be stopped by Restraint as God is humanity's questioning of metaphysically sanctioned limits and the human push for the exercise of freedom within the context of responsible membership in community. While human efforts to this end are usually frustrated, the building project continues, and it does so without reliance on the idea of God. In fact, it requires the rejection of the symbol God, and humanism serves as a fitting eulogy for God's demise.

Good-bye God

How many times have you heard from progressive theists something along the lines of "we can't understand God's plan"? Or, "God understands our pain in this moment and will work justice?"

Lodged in such responses is an age-old assumption that suffering can produce larger, positive consequences on both the personal and communal level. Too much attention to stories such as that of Nimrod or the highlighting of the death of Jesus the Christ as clear markers of the relationship between suffering and spiritual renewal has produced this almost knee jerk reaction to the absurdity of violence and destruction. I understand the desire for meaning, the yearning for purpose even in the most horrific of events. Humans by their very nature seek connections, push for meaning, but this turn to a cosmic force clouds ability to fully grasp the nature of human tragedy and hampers robust effort to make a difference to the extent there is a tendency to await "a word from the Lord." This is not a loss of faith, but rather it is recognition of the limits of faith in the face of tragedy.

What is so important, what is so impressive, is not faithful appeals to God but rather collective human effort to comfort those most directly impacted by this event and to remember the value of human life. Trying to resolve tragedies and keep God on the throne actually hampers ability to process misery because it is given through appeal to God's logic some type of cosmic cover that is difficult to remove.

It seems to me, as we read the stories of the victims—those destroyed in the Bible, like those who followed Nimrod—we are also reading God's obituary. By this I mean such extreme human tragedy makes it impossible to talk about God in any useful way.

Do not read this statement as a selfish demand for comfort, for an easy life. No, it is recognition that nothing explains away the destruction of life's integrity; but instead it highlights the fact that we labor in this world without cosmic aid that can protect us from us. Appeals to free will—as my comments are bound to generate—might not be a limitation God imposes on God's self.

It may simply be a weak way of saying we are in control—to the extent control can be claimed.

Tragedy slowly kills God, making it so difficult, if not useless, to speak of God in response to misery. Silence. Deep silence, in which we struggle for human resolve to confront human problems.

Please do not misunderstand me: I am not saying we should say nothing, that we should do nothing. I am not suggesting that complacency is the proper response, nor am I arguing that these events should be ignored. Rather, I am saying silence concerning God, silence concerning efforts to make things better through theological twist and turns—through the revamping of experience to fit religious categories and religious tradition.

This is not to say that humanists have all the answers. Rather, humanists might offer better questions during challenging times, as well as a space for wrestling with these questions free of cosmic justifications and a God clearly missing in action despite what God's advocates might provide as theological spin. God is not present; instead these stories like that of Nimrod speak of God's absence. Once more, they write God's obituary. The good news in the face of this loss: fragile, uncertain, and inconsistent fellow human travelers are present.

6

Humanism and the rethinking of a King's King

In the previous chapter, I offered a deconstruction of the idea of God in light of humanist principles and practices emerging in the work of Nimrod. It was a way of bringing humanists into the biblical story. But here, in the second chapter of Section two, I want to explore how humanism might serve to modify the notion of God for theists in ways that decrease the ethical harm theism enacts in the world. That is to say, if theism is not going away—and I do not think it is—how might humanist thinking serve to make it less toxic to human life?

I answer this question by tackling what I consider one of the most perplexing and damaging theological-philosophical questions aping theistic orientations such as Christianity. That question is the problem of moral evil, particularly as it is framed in terms of theodicy: what can one say about God in light of suffering in the world? Responses to theodical constructions of suffering tend to endorse suffering as meritorious.

As surfaced but not fully addressed in the last chapter, I have for some time held a deep appreciation for the weight of moral evil as theological and philosophical problem, particularly as related to the history of responses to this dilemma articulated by African Americans.[1] Most notably, I have lamented, interrogated, and challenged any reliance on redemptive suffering argumentation as the linchpin of theodical reflection.[2] In earlier texts, I at times painted Martin Luther King Jr.'s theodicy the twentieth-century standard for the redemptive suffering approach. And, in this chapter, he continues to serve as a significant case study—one useful in modifying divine activity and accountability within the world.

The following pages afford me an opportunity to once again (but from a different angle) think through this topic of response to moral evil. While

I called for the demise of God (as Restraint) earlier, I here work based on another consideration: What might humanism offer those who have not yet surrendered God, but have some liberal sensibilities at work in their theological-philosophical thinking?

This undertaking is twofold: reexamination of my early perspective on the issue of God and moral evil as well as explication of particular dimensions of King's theological purview. Put in the form of a question, what might we say about moral evil and the Divine if King's theology and humanism are brought together? While wrestling with this question, I give attention to four thematic concerns:

1 "somebodyness" and the theological significance of the body;
2 King and the Personal God;
3 Reenvisioning the Divine; and
4 Divine mishaps and detours.

At its core this chapter is heuristic in nature, involving speculation on the potential for synergy between King's thought—his Personalist doctrine of God and concern for embodiment as marker of progress—and less marginal elements of humanist sensibilities such as a robust anthropology and what I will call a hermeneutic of life.[3] For some, this project involves at least a seemingly odd combination to be sure, yet these perspectives are in fact connected already.

The basic principles of King's Personalism and the basic assumptions of humanism are lodged firmly within a larger and contiguous tradition of liberal religious thought with, I would argue, at least subtle connections to particular modes of humanism (e.g., Ethical Culture). Hence, they share an intellectual context and neither is an imposition over against the religious leanings of many groups. Furthermore, on a fundamental level they resonate with a fundamental ethical framework in that they both maintain social consciousness—a recognition that life lived must involve a push for greater options and integrity, whether one calls this push "freedom" or "liberation" is of little consequence. In a word, although appealing to different segments of complex communities, both are organic and reflect a passionate commitment (expressed rhetorically) to social transformation and communal growth marked by justice.[4]

"Somebodyness" and the theological significance of the body

In spite of persistent evil that challenged what he assumed was God's intentions for God's people, King maintained a perception of ultimate good—of a teleological sense of history—put in place and guided by a personal God. While this position "preached" (and continues to "preach") well and served as a source of moral and ethical determination, in light of persistent moral evil it frames one of the strongest theological-philosophical challenges: Moral evil housed within the continuing struggle for life as signification of liberation discourse. Yet, perhaps in part this dilemma stems from a misread of what is most theologically valuable about King's view on the religious underpinning and theological signs of progress.

A careful read of King's theological insights suggests the manner in which the human body itself provides compelling evidence of progress toward liberation. But this requires a delicate theological balance: Too much attention to the value of the body can result in the type of humanism King feared and rejected. Too little attention to the value of the body as benchmark of God's activity can result in a groundless and romantic faith that forfeits any sense of the world's importance—an otherworldly orientation that does not push for felt change within our historical moment. Over against the latter King's approach promotes aesthetic considerations as theological insight, thereby highlighting the vitality of embodiment.

"Somebodyness" conceptually grounds King's method, and it bears both theological and existential significance in that it suggests an alternate placement of bodies (in this case, black bodies) in time and space—a rethinking of the dual nature of the body—as symbol and as biochemical reality. The body takes on a new meaning, a new value, and a new importance that trump troubled historical relations. God provides resources for the revitalization of the *imago Dei*—the reviving of the human—as new perception of the body's meaning and historical placement.

The demand for sociopolitical and economic restructuring is only the residue of this revamping of human *being* in that it is first measured by an increased sense of complex subjectivity couched in acknowledgment of the black body's radiant beauty. In the words of a popular religious song, "I looked at my hands and they looked new. I looked at my feet and they did too" and in King's words:

> This sense of **somebodyness** means the refusal to be ashamed of being black. Our children must be taught to stand tall with their heads proudly lifted. We need not be duped into purchasing bleaching creams that promise to make us lighter. We need not process our hair to make it appear straight. Whether some men, black and white, realize it or not, black people are very beautiful. . . . The Negro, through self-acceptance and self-appreciation, will one day cause white America to see that integration is not an obstacle, but an opportunity to participate in the beauty of diversity.[5]

"Somebodyness" as theological concept promotes dynamic embodiment as the proper response to moral evil. That is to say, opposition to moral evil understood as the warping of humanity involves a reconstituting of the human. "With this new sense of 'somebodyness' and self-respect," King recounts, "a new Negro has emerged with a new determination to achieve freedom and human dignity whatever the cost may be. This is the true meaning of the struggle that is taking place in the south today."[6] Again, aesthetic transformation vis-à-vis "somebodyness" and a new ontology are followed in time by felt and functional shifts in sociopolitical and economic reality. And the ultimate triumph of God's will in human history is known through the placement of these reconstituted bodies in the "Beloved Community."

King and the Personal God

Tied to this theological anthropology is doctrine of God developed within academic reflection and church-based praxis. In the final analysis King held to a radical sense of optimism in the face of profound suffering, but wrestled with the proper correlation between God's power and purpose in human history.[7] We might say that, in a real way, he came to rest theologically on a notion of God's power as "sufficient power to accomplish the most noble ends or purposes in cooperation with created persons."[8] Couched in this stance is a shift away from strict omnipotence to an understanding of God as having "matchless power."[9] In other words and in light of continuing existential realities, God's power is best understood as entailing ability beyond that of humans, but it is not a traditional sense of God's power as limitless. The goodness, love, righteousness, and so on that characterize God for most African American Christian theists remain intact for King. Yet, the manner in which they are expressed in human history is reconsidered. What is more, King's sense of God and God's presence in the world necessitate attention to the body as both a gauge of change and a tool of transformation. In a word, King's God, as civil rights activism makes clear, requires human participation in order to bring about the "good."

As a humanist, I can appreciate this taming of the God concept in ways that foster accountability and responsibility on the part of humans—through an appeal to the dignity of personality. Yet, it disappoints my humanist sensibilities in that such a reformulation does not provide necessarily a sustainable shift away from the dilemma of redemptive suffering. That is to say, it does not preclude the possibility of collective suffering (e.g., racism and sexism) having secondary benefit—a kind of "no cross, no crown" perspective. King preaches and promotes the importance of the human person, but not in a way that allows for tenaciously safeguarding said body against unmerited sufferings. To the contrary, pain endured is often noted as a mechanism for refining the human. In this regard, King's theology might be said to simply affirm a long tradition of redemptive suffering argumentation that litters the religious/theological geography of African American communities. This, however, is not the only option when reading King.

What if one gives center stage to a sometimes minority perspective within King's thought? What if one were to highlight the theological posture with which King flirted as a student, that of his Boston University professor Edgar Brightman? According to Brightman, God can "actualize the good," this remains the domain of the Divine, but this ability does not preclude shifts in plan and strategy on the part of God. The purpose in breaking into human history, as many theologians want to put it, remains clearly focused on the good. This theological posture, however, prioritizes God's overall agenda, not every divine action and maneuver found within that large framework. And in this way, God's power does not prevent missteps and wrong turns (albeit even these point to God's deep desire to help humanity). Penultimate events related to God's agenda are not guaranteed effective. Such a shift in stance regarding the work of the divine is significant within theistic contexts in which the mind of God and God's activities were always considered complete, while not always discernable to people.

Humans also fall short at times, willing evil rather than good. In this sense, for instance, King might explain the failed Albany (Georgia) campaign as one such move, a strategy that did not point to ultimate failure of "right" over "evil," but rather a moment during which the partnership between humans and God did not bear fruit. This alternate reading, I believe, is, let us say, a big (theological/philosophical) deal.

The above involves a restructuring of God's power in ways that not only allows for maintenance of the God concept but also recognizes shortcomings in Divine interaction with humans. In the context of this chapter, such a theological understanding points to missteps and not a fundamental questioning of the Divine. This is because these missteps are followed by new strategies and maneuvers. God is still concerned with the good because a racist deity, one could argue, would exercise power in a more consistently demonic manner and this would be present in the development of human history. Yet, the limits entailed mean no longer thinking about God as "King" or Lord of the Universe in the same, old, theological ways.

Such a shift in doctrine of God, combined with humanist sensibilities, may offer a way to maintain theistic commitments without a glorification of human suffering as redemptive. That is to say, one can continue to claim God is loving, kind, just, and committed to the welfare of those who suffer. Here is the difference: Many theologians have assumed, however, that this assortment of characteristics necessitates an understanding that all events enacted by such a God must lead directly to the desired end. Even King notes that God is the best example of personality, of action, and of faithfulness.[10] Nonetheless, for King, this involves the best of these traits, not the perfection of these traits. In a word, God—even as "matchless" in character and capability—may shift perspective, change direction, "repent" for decisions made without losing status as the best knower and doer—the ultimate source of our understanding of freedom and the framework for our sense of relationship and community (as "Beloved Community").

In light of this, I cannot resist raising a question: What might be the look of liberal theologies if they were to take seriously the type of God concept opened through King's theology, and use it to interrogate continuing modalities of discrimination?

Reenvisioning the Divine

These liberal theologies maintain recognition of moral evil as real and felt—as a problem. And they are clear on the role of humans in perpetuating this problem. The challenge, however, has involved the best way to theologically place God in relationship to this moral evil. It is in regard to this sticking point that the Christ Event is viewed by many liberal theologians as having deep and lasting significance. To be sure, in some significant ways such theologies are an extended Christology. Such a privileging of the Christ Event not only frames these theological discourses but also troubles these discourses in that the cross follows close on the heels of a revolutionary ministry.

Let us take one theologian as an example of this issue. Kelly Brown Douglas, who was trained by the founder of liberation theology within African American communities—James Cone—, argues God was opposed to the crucifixion of Christ but did not (or could not?) stop it.[11] Furthermore, God's answer to suffering is found not in the pain of Christ but in the triumph of the resurrection. Humans, on the other hand, are responsible for the death of Christ. When considered this way, a question is unavoidable: "is there any positive, empowering value for a suffering people to be found in a religion with an unjust execution at its center?" Douglas's response: "I contend that there is."[12] Douglas does not render the act of suffering privileged experience; rather, she couches suffering in deep meaning by giving the body of those who suffer status as "vessels for God's revelation concerning the value of human life and concomitantly the character of God's power." Questions concerning the power of God are sidestepped and the Christ Event, understood using a hermeneutic of appropriation, is said to highlight God's appreciation for humanity through the "reclamation of it" after the crucifixion.[13] A dilemma remains and haunting questions abound: Is this stance sufficient? And, what does the cross really specify?

In light of the Christ Event, to continue to speak of God and all this commitment implies must entail for justice-minded theologians' recognition of both death and life. The latter is present in vibrant ways in their theology, and death too—but only as the precursor to a continuing transcendence—the removal of God in order for God to reappear. This, however, has done little to address fundamental problems related to moral evil and theodicy. And typical responses—beyond silence—entail talk of God in louder terms, as if volume and passion can substitute for substance and historically situated presence.

"Death of God" theologians like Thomas J. J. Altizer, it seems, tried to address such dilemmas by claims that God is "dead." While many theologians would find such a pronouncement unacceptable (God is Dead?), they would, I believe, agree with the notion that God allows God's self to be absorbed into the world for humanity's sake. By this attention grabbing statement he meant in the Christ Event God completely empties God's self into the world, and the spirit of God is not resurrected but defused through the world.[14]

The proposition that God kills God-self in the Christ Event is a work of theodicy meant to explain an apparent silence in the face of moral evil. In short, in killing God's self, God has done the work for us, saving us from the task but does this offer us anything substantive in terms of our moral evil dilemma? Based on continued oppression faced by many, did God's plan for improvement fail? God's self-sacrifice did not stem the tide of destruction. God remains good and just—traits of central importance—but has taken a tact that in fact has done little to change the plight of African Americans who continue to suffer. Was the Christ Event the final word, or even a proper word?

Liberal, social transformation committed theologians will want to follow him only so far on this path in that what Altizer pushed for does not recognize the demonic nature of oppression, oppression that blocks this unity between God and world.[15] What might offend such theologians in particular and liberal Christians in general is not the process of God's emptying into the world, rather it is the language used to describe this event. God is infused in human history through Christ, and humans participate in this divinity to the extent they take on—in an ontological sense—God's character. The Divine is submerged in the context of human suffering and in so doing removes the transcendent element: God emptied God's self and imploded transcendence for the sake of humanity.

Divine mishaps and detours

Perhaps the notion of "divine mishaps and detours" is the best available way of addressing the dilemmas raised above. Yet, what might be most objectionable about this theological stance is the manner in which it entertains, no requires, an acceptance of a God whose plan develops in awkward and bulky stages, in fits and starts. This God takes sides and is concerned with liberation. It is not the motivation or commitment of this God that is questioned; rather, it is recognition that this God's activities are incomplete. This God's work is incomplete, or flawed in part because this God's liberative work is experimental—changing and often reactive, demonstrating commitment and concern but guaranteeing little. This God interacts with humans in ways involving self-correction, changed plans and paths. God according to this scheme is deeply attached to and committed to the welfare of humanity—but perhaps at times through penultimate events that fail to suggest an ultimate and positive resolution.

In terms of application, this stance involves an alternate perspective on Christology through acknowledgment of the Christ Event as penultimate, as a marker of God's posture toward the world as opposed to being a conclusive response to modern modalities of oppression. The Christ Event has limited constructive reach. The Event was incomplete, inconclusive, serving as a marker of God's ability and commitment unfulfilled in our historical moment. And an embrace of it by liberal Christians might be seen as entailing an act of faith, but not as traditionally perceived. Faith here involves moving through the world as if God has already acted again—living in anticipation of continued activity on the part of God, activity that will be significant.

There is another dimension to it in that faith involves a matter of action in light of dynamic faith: Theists forgiving God for God's miscalculation. How is forgiveness the proper way to frame human posture toward God? Moral evil is not simply free will out of control; current circumstances also arise from miscalculation on God's part. It is not to say that God cannot be held accountable because God is not omnipotent. Rather, God is held accountable not because God did not act but because God's actions simply shifted the problem. God's approach has not worked, if liberation (as black theology suggests) is the norm. Hence, God's good intentions must be recognized and the shortcomings of God's activity noted without resentment. In so doing dynamic forgiveness is exercised: dynamic because it is infused with a strong sense of purpose and a matter of forgiveness in that it entails behavior interrogated and pardoned. In a certain way this is a pointing out of a hopeful emptiness, of absence but in ways that call for humans to fill the void as best they can. Doctrine of God becomes anthropology writ large. This is what the Christ Event might mean when King's theology and my humanist sensibilities are brought together.

7

Putting Jesus in his place

Having addressed God in two ways, a turn to the embodiment of the divine/human relationship is a next logical step for humanism concerned with engaging fundamental elements of the dominant modality of theism within the United States—the Christian faith. Mindful of this, here I wrestle with another nagging element of the Christian Trinity—Jesus "the Christ."[1] And, I do so mindful of the focus of this section as well as that of the first: Is there anything gained through attention to Jesus? Does he help to address racism and, as a religious figure, give meaning to life? My answer of course is "no" to both questions, and what follows is the reason for that response.

What would Jesus do?

The history of white supremacy in the United States and the struggle against the ramifications of that history have in part been worked out through the meaning of Jesus' physical presence on earth. And this presence involves an aesthetic of physical and spiritual beauty as well as a system of ethics ("What would Jesus do?"). I argue that efforts to challenge whiteness as normative through the aesthetics presented in the story of Jesus's "look" and through efforts to mimic Jesus's system of ethics fall short. This is because they are based on biblical mythology that can be manipulated and made to support any position on whiteness. That is to say, a positive blackness based on Jesus Christ's person and ethics does little to challenge a positive whiteness. The symbolic importance of Jesus' life and ministry can be used to support either a critique of whiteness discourse or an embrace of it. In this regard Jesus is a fluid symbol, taking any shape necessary.

Furthermore, both discourses of whiteness and discourses of blackness are too limiting in that both present limited ways to identify one's humanity. In either case, one's humanity is recognized only to the extent it can be defined by this one marker of life meaning. More to the point, both fail to wrestle with the fundamental nature of moral evil—a denial of the right to physically and discursively occupy time and space in complex and transformative ways. Whiteness and blackness both limit identity and humanity by limiting the self (and the self in relationship to others) to racialized depictions of the embodied person. Instead of attempting to counter the damage down by whiteness discourse through a claiming of Jesus's blackness—either as a symbolic "more" or ethical mandate—it is vital to recognize the limits of Christology (i.e., study of Jesus the Christ) as a model for human self-understanding. That is to say, Christology demonstrates the limits of scripturally based understandings of humanity and makes room for humanism.

Using Jesus

White supremacy made connections to the Christ Event—but did so with the force of historically manifest dominance: Those of European descent, the story goes, must have a deep relationship to Christ (and God through Christ) in that they have been given dominance over the land and those who dwell in the land. In this regard, the appeal of enslaved Africans (and their descendants) to a special relationship with Christ based on shared knowledge of suffering and kinship is challenged by theological workings buttressed by sociopolitical and economic dominance. While not making this statement regarding the relationship of white supremacy to Jesus Christ, Stephen Prothero's take on the growing significance of Jesus in early US religious history is telling. "In the early nineteenth century," Prothero writes, "evangelicals liberated Jesus first from Calvinism and then from creeds. Though few rejected his divinity, Americans emphasized his humanity, transforming him from a distant god in a complex theological system into a near-and-dear person, fully embodied, with virtues they could imitate, mind they could understand, and qualities they could love."[2] At times in the history of the United States and for various reasons, Christ would be disassociated with the more rigid interpretations of the Christian faith and narrow readings of the scripture.

Jesus became approachable or within the epistemological and ethical grasp of typical Americans.[3] What is more, white supremacy's rehearsal of partnership with Christ also includes an assumption of aesthetic similarity: Christ looks European. Christ in the world was a plastic symbol—capable of alteration and movement, no fixed shape or time as discourse concerning the implications of Christ shifted in harmony with altered sociopolitical, economic, and cultural realities. In this way, the ability of Jesus to speak to a particular age, the growth of the United States, required presentation consistent with the aesthetic sensibilities of that age.

If not an accurate depiction of the physical "look" of the dominant voices and figures of this age, images of Christ—such as Warner Sallman's "The Head of Christ"—presented Christ constant with an idyllic or iconic image in line with the preferences of many within that age. There are ways in which depictions of Christ—visual images of Jesus Christ—promoted a particular social cohesiveness and sense of collective identity on the cultural-political level.[4] Yet, such images promoted more than a sociopolitical imaginary in that they also spoke to the proper "look" of a citizen, the racially visible markers of belonging. In this regard, one can stretch out the chronology of Christ imagery by which the meaning of the nineteenth-century hymn, "More Like Jesus," involves a type of normative gaze whereby the indwelling of Christ ethically arranged is deeply associated with the embodied body. In the materiality of the human body in the world is found the presence and meaning of Jesus Christ:

> More like Jesus would I be, let my Savior dwell with me;
> Fill my soul with peace and love—make me gentle as a dove;
> More like Jesus, while I go, pilgrim in this world below;
> Poor in spirit would I be; let my Savior dwell in me.[5]

In addition to the above, it is also the case that this aesthetic of divinity—*imago Dei*—as represented by Christ also legitimizes a moral and ethical posture toward the world, a particular sense of the public sphere and proper involvement in it. In other words, through the visual image is communicated—with transfixed and a rendered troupe of relationship—civil religion tied to a particular "look" and connection to the dominant life imagery.[6]

This tangling of body aesthetics depicted within the context of a transfiguration of Christ is not unique to those in North America. The history of religious art shows variation based on sensitivity to sociocultural assumptions—in some cases a muscular Jesus trumps a more slender depiction, for example. But the European masters of the art world depicted Christ consistent with the "look" of their communities. But why this significance accorded images? "The significance and power of popular religious imagery," writes David Morgan, "resides precisely in its contribution to the social construction of reality, whether in the everyday domain of visual and epistemological recipes that guide people through the day or the liminal passages of crisis and transformation that dramatically shape their lives." He continues, "Worlds are composed of both the ordinary and the extraordinary, and images serve to configure each aspect of experience."[7] The image—in this case of Christ—becomes natural,[8] affirming and representative of the communal aesthetics supporting a particular ethics of life and accompanying interaction with the world. And, while images of Christ clearly played out social anxieties over the nature and meaning of gender, as both Morgan and Prothero note, they also—both explicitly and implicitly—made a statement concerning the racial ordering of life in the United States. In this way, the masculine and race-based matrix of "life and liberty" in the United States had not only the force of law (and social custom) but also divine sanction based on the physical look of God's presence in the world. Said plainly, God resembles in flesh those whom God favors. At times, in the context of race relations in the United States, this has meant the imagining of God through Christ as divine sanction of white superiority as both material and ontological family resemblance.

The depiction of Jesus Christ is tied to sociopolitical and economic conversations and needs. And the imaginary of Christ alters with the demands and concerns of shifting cultural worlds. "Within this constantly reconnoitered terrain," writes David Morgan, "the body and its genders are politically contested and the identity of Jesus is as varied and unstable as the history of the search for him."[9] And here is the key: "The devout seek in his depictions an image of what they wish the world to be."[10] And white Americans were not alone in working through a vast array of issues and concerns vis-à-vis the imagining of Christ. They were not alone in reconfiguring the image of Christ to give religious-theological sanction to the aesthetics of identity formation.

Black folks and a Jesus who understands "Us"

African Americans meant Christology and imaginaries of Christ in particular as both response to the above circumstances and also as a creative effort to craft themselves in light of their own understanding of the Christian faith. Early discussions and depictions of Jesus Christ within certain strands of African American imagination did not necessarily fix on the physical presentation of Christ as similar to that of enslaved Africans. Instead, much more emphasis was given to a shared image based on ethics and epistemology both meant to short-circuit white supremacy and advance African American self-understanding.

The Christological emphasis in certain geographies of African American religion begins early. Our ability to date this presence is hampered greatly by a lack of records, but surviving cultural production attests to the significance of Jesus Christ as ideological partner, epistemological kin, and ethical guide. Starting with the spirituals, enslaved Africans measured the terror and absurdity of their world over against the cultural world inhabited by Jesus and by his response to that world. In certain respects, Jesus Christ served as symbol and troupe working against the dehumanization of enslaved existence. If enslavement represents a form of social death, as Orlando Patterson argues, Jesus Christ provided a reconstituted self through the details of his life and resurrection.[11] Time and historical context, in this instance, give way to the pain shared by the righteous and the empathy of God toward those faced with existential angst and embodied pain. Jesus and enslaved Africans share knowledge:

> Don't ever feel discouraged
> For Jesus is your friend
> And if you lack of knowledge
> He'll ne'er refuse to lend.[12]

The idea that enslaved Africans are adrift, detangled from the workings of cultural worlds that once sustained them, or as they sang—"some times I feel like a motherless child, along ways from home"—is matched by a counter force of familiarity with a cosmic force having significant power and capacity:

> Ride on King Jesus!
> No man can hinder him
> Ride on King Jesus!
> No man can hinder him

And,

> I was young when I begun
> No man can hinder him
> But now my race is almost run
> No man can hinder him.[13]

Compassion and power in a historically targeted pattern are highlighted within the context of the spirituals, as enslaved Africans and their descendants work through the trauma and joys of life within the confines of their life geographies.

Little attention in this early Christology is given to the biological reality of Jesus the Christ; instead, enslaved Africans emphasized his relationship to suffering humanity and consequential demands for justice. In general, the color of Jesus was of less importance, a lesser marker of the value of black (enslaved) bodies, than was a shared relationship to God: both Jesus and enslaved Africans marked out the reality (in differing ways of course) of the *imago Dei*. Hence, it is the connection through creation and suffering that signified their condition and the theological logic justifying their oppression. So, Jesus was their kin, not necessarily through his looks but clearly in knowledge and the context of misery.

> Nobody knows de trouble I've had
> Nobody knows but Jesus
> Nobody know de trouble I've had
> Glory, hallelu![14]

The Jesus Event presents a moral compass and an ethical posture toward the world that serves the enslaved, helping them recognize the manner in which Jesus Christ presents both the form and content of transformed existence. As the spiritual proclaims:

> Children Jesus died to set me free
> Nailed to that cross on Calvary[15]

African Americans expressed this perspective with regard to the shared epistemology of suffering that marked the Christ Event and the nature of enslavement. By making this link, it was possible to expose the claims of white Americans to Christ as involving political maneuvering and mundane economics as the residue of white supremacy rhetoric covered by theological claims.

When Jesus becomes black

Theological rhetoric from the period of slavery forward spoke to this assumption and tied it to the transformation of the public arena and sociopolitical interactions on interpersonal levels. "The fact that black people in the United States had not been destroyed by slavery," writes minister Alexander Crummell, "demonstrated that the sufferings of the 'captive exiles from Africa' were meant not as a judgment but as a discipline. Their tribulations were not intended to punish or destroy but to prepare the black race for a glorious destiny."[16] In this way, blackness over against whiteness and theologized white supremacy becomes the marker of national salvation. The illusion to the Christ Event as redemption rather than merited punishment is telling. Note the above quotation in comparison with this biblical statement often used by Christians to describe the Messiah: "But he was wounded for our transgressions; he was crushed for our iniquities; upon him was the chastisement that brought us peace, and with his stripes we are healed."[17] By tying redemption to the workings of black embodied bodies, African American religious rhetoric often countered the biblical basis for discriminatory social arrangements.

Related to the above, the typical read of the story of Ham (i.e., the Genesis account of the curse on Canaan) supports whiteness as marker of divine favor and in connection to this, it assumes that there is a theological link between blackness and divine displeasure. However, some African American religious leaders, such as James Theodore Holly, signified this reading of Genesis and instead argued that the salvific act found in the Christ Event runs through the redemptive qualities of the Hamadic line of peoples. Blackness (as Ham is said to be the ancestor of Africans) becomes a symbol of existential and ontological merit to the extent it marks the people through whom God works in the world. Furthermore, Simon the Cyrenian's carrying the cross for Jesus the Christ as he is marched to his death gives Simon and his black descendants a special place with Christ. Thereby salvation history holds the marks of "ethnological development."[18] Assuming the reality of the groupings presented in Genesis, Holly argues:

> The converted Ethiopian eunuch, as well as Simon the Cyrenian, who carried Christ's cross, and the Canaanitish woman whose faith our Lord declared to have been greater than any He had found in Israel, all go to show how the descendants of Ham continued to mingle in the designs of Almighty God down to the development of the Gospel dispensation. Hence, it may appear that the Semitic race has given us the written thought of God's Divine Plan; the Japhetic race has openly proclaimed this thought in the printed and preached WORD; but both alike await the forthcoming ministry of the Hamitic race to reduce to practical ACTION that spoken word, that written thought.[19]

Put differently, blackness is the mark of Christ's salvific work in the world; and in this way, African Americans bear the marks of Christ and serve as a symbol of God's ongoing presence in the world. Such a formulation involves the messianic quality of individuals who come to represent visually the personification of Christ's character and ethics.

Perhaps most notable within this robust Christology is the unapologetic embrace of Jesus Christ as not only sympathetic to the plight of God's "dark" children but Jesus Christ as embodying blackness. In this way, *imago Dei* gains greater political meaning within the discourse of race in that it provides theological rationale for the full humanity and social importance of African Americans.[20] It bridges visual worlds in that *imago Dei* comes to connote both a metaphysical "truth" and a historical/physical mandate. Thereby work within the world and visualization of this world entails something of both cosmic and mundane significance—dismantling the divide between the "sacred" and the "secular" because both are recognized as the symbolism of Jesus Christ. Christology is intertwined with anthropology, as they are mutually dependent.

While implied in the doctrine of God offered by figures such as Henry McNeal Turner ("God Is a Negro"), it is with the mid-twentieth century that the physical representation of Jesus Christ as black gains its most significant ground. Deep within the civil rights movement was a vision of renewed life based upon the demise of white supremacy and the rise of humanity recognized beyond the superficial markers of racial and ethnic difference. And for Christians seeking to articulate this new vision, the rethinking of Christ imagery was a necessity. Whereas Henry McNeal Turner softens his polemical proclamation of God as black by offering a preference for the color of God more deeply associated with the colors of the natural world—if whites will also release God from their image—some within the civil rights era and post civil rights black consciousness ideology reclaimed the blackness of Christ as epistemological, ontological, and political reality. The notion of "black is beautiful" was brought to bear on the aesthetics of political life as well as serving as a hermeneutic by which to strip away whiteness (and all its implications) from the metaphysical under pinning of Christian life. In this way, an effort was made to foster a theological aesthetic for various modalities of black identity within the context of a rhetorically Christian nation. The liberation of African Americans oppressed through the workings of white supremacy required this reclaiming of Christ.

Gone was the blonde hair and blue eyes. In their place, an afro, brown skin and brown eyes: one was more likely to see the children of Christ in the troubled terrain of inner city communities than in carefully crafted suburban communities. More and more churches visually presented Christ as black—the same positioning of Christ (with the disciplines, in the Garden of Gethsemane, and so on) but without the physically represented assumption of whiteness. Not all preaching and physical church structures embraced this move, but enough did and did so in light of a growingly radical theological conversation.

The challenge to both the physical and epistemological whiteness of Christ is given its strongest theological articulation in late-twentieth-century discourses growing out of liberal religion and political justice campaigns. Whereas figures such as the late Reverend Albert Cleage (Jaramogi Abebe Agyeman), pastor of the Shrine of the Black Madonna, argued for the physical blackness of Jesus Christ—the black revolutionary whose recorded perspectives and opinions nurture the late-twentieth-century black Christian nationalist impulse—most African American theologies are less concerned with physical blackness as the primary marker of importance. "Although Jesus' ethnicity and dark-skinned complexion are certainly important aspects of Christ's blackness," writes theologian Kelly Brown Douglas, "to call Christ

Black points to more than simply ancestry or biological characteristics."[21] A sense of God as being ontologically black,[22] working through Christ, suggests an image of Christ as connected to the liberative impulse of African American communities—embodied within their very struggle for social transformation. "What does Jesus Christ mean for the oppressed blacks of the land?" ask theologian James Cone.[23] And the answer: Christ must be removed from images of a white Jesus meant to safeguard white supremacy. Instead, for African Americans, the Christ imaginary must entail the depiction of him as "the Oppressed One" who struggles on behalf of African Americans to bring about a situation marked by transformed existence. In other words, "In a society that defines blackness as evil and whiteness as good, the theological significance of Jesus is found in the possibility of human liberation through blackness. Jesus is the black Christ!"[24] Theologian J. Deotis Roberts, among others, noted the manner in which Christ must be free from reified and limiting notions of incarnation, and instead must be recognized as bearing in his actions and commitments the full range of humanity. Cone, however, understood late-twentieth-century blackness (in association with black power) as the paradigmatic status of Christ.

Jesus the Christ is black for Cone, but this involves not so much a biological statement as much as it is an epistemological and ethical statement—meaning Jesus Christ is known visually through the placement of black bodies in time and space, and is present wherever effort is made to fight racism and challenge white supremacy's basic assumptions. The logic here involves a redefining of blackness over against whiteness whereby the former becomes the basic hermeneutic of life meaning in the United States. It supersedes discourses of whiteness as the language of American life and thought. Even negative reaction against this depiction of Christ points to the problematic assumptions of whiteness guiding thought and action in the United States. "The same white theologians," writes Cone, "who laughingly dismiss Albert Cleage's 'Black Messiah' say almost nothing about the European (white) images of Christ plastered all over American homes and churches. I perhaps would respect the integrity of their objections to the Black Christ on scholarly grounds, if they applied the same vigorous logic to Christ's whiteness, especially in contexts where his blackness is not advocated."[25]

Hip-hop Jesus

Perhaps the most radical depiction of Jesus without whiteness is found in hip-hop culture—particularly in the look and meaning of who Tupac Shakur references as "Black Jesus." Tupac's Jesus is the patron saint of thugs who shapes life transformation vis-à-vis conversion as a shift that respects the realities of urban life and upholds the values and morality of survival within the harsh realities of existence.[26] Such a religious-theological move as advocated by Tupac does not entail surrender to absurdity, a morphing into an unrecognizable connection to the absurd. Rather, the convert's Black Jesus has a posture toward the world involving the movement of the trickster, not the traditional Christ. The trickster recognizes and signifies life arrangements that trouble most—pushing for a more vibrant existence that does not fear the world. Tupac speaks to this when saying, "he's our saint that we pray to; that we look up to. Drug dealers, they sinning, right? But they'll be millionaires. How I got shot five times—only a saint, only Black Jesus, only a nigga that know where I'm coming from, could be, like, 'You know what? He's gonna end up doing some good'."[27] Such a resolution—"He's gonna end up doing some good."—mirrors the workings of the Black Jesus, rendering Tupac and those like him—thugs—followers of Jesus who, through their actions in the world, live out the precepts of their faith. As the lyrics to the aptly titled track "Blasphemy" attest: "They say Jesus is a kind man, well he should understand times in this crime land, my Thug nation."[28] At times, Black Jesus is not a distant figure, a removed and foreign being. Instead, there are times during which one is led to believe Tupac is Black Jesus—a transfiguration of Christ whereby the marks of the biblically articulated crucifixion are replaced with tattoos as the markings of Christ's sacrifice. With Tupac, Christ not only takes on the look and sensibilities of African Americans. Instead, the imaginary of Christ becomes associated with a dimension of black life troubling to whiteness and certain formations of African American identity. Jesus Christ, that is to say, becomes associated with the "least of these" in a very different way—with bling and the markings of hip-hop aesthetics.

Reformulations of Christology in black trouble the dominance of whiteness as normative representative of the ideal human in relationship to ontological depth. However, this is done in a way that also reenforces the masculine or gendered nature of normative visions of human engagement with the divine as well as the most productive arrangement of ethnical engagement between humans regarding pressing issues. This sense of the visual representation of Christ (within the context of historical and contemporary community) as black based on a set of sociopolitical, economic, and cultural markers damages the theological undergirding of white supremacy while also, at its best, allowing for attention to the challenges of gender found in any attempt to "depict" Christ. For theologian Jacquelyn Grant, the reality of Jesus is experiential in nature—based on the ability of Jesus to dwell where suffering women are and respond to their plight with transformative possibilities. In a word, "Black women's affirmation of Jesus as God meant that White people were not God."[29] Through the insightful and sharp critique of theologians such as

Grant, many of whom were trained by Cone, blackness was freed from the assumption of masculinity. Or, in the words of Kelly Brown Douglas, "The Black Christ explicitly disavows White oppression of Black people. The problem is that it does not go beyond that. It does not portray the complexity of Black oppression. Specifically, it does not address the fact that Black people oppress each other, and that racism is not the only barrier to Black freedom."[30] In a word, visualization of a black Jesus did not, of necessity, involve denouncement of sexism. In this regard, the image of Christ for many scholars revolves around ethics—what did/would Jesus do, as opposed to the look of the historical Jesus. Hence, Jesus is paradigmatic representation of embodied activity in the world. Therefore, Jesus Christ occupies the bodies of those who work for fullness of life, for a complex array of life options.

This does not rule out the possibility of depicting Jesus Christ as visual and culturally black (male or female), but it does deny the ability of any one transfiguration of Christ to serve as normative. Jesus Christ as the embodied and visual presence of transformative ethics is given priority.[31] Images mark the plastic nature of expression and the shifting "look" of existential need. Yet, even these various efforts to rework Jesus the Christ have left in place difficulties that raise questions regarding the utility of Christ imagery.

The dilemma of Christology

Christology has been a mainstay of Christian thought; in fact, it has been the central theological category used to frame the nature and meaning of human engagement with/in the world. However, this has come at a cost. In what remains of this chapter I address briefly several of the problems associated with this reliance on Christology: (1) the normalizing of human suffering vis-à-vis a mythology of external redemptive mechanisms; (2) persistent shadow presence of whiteness as the framework for African American self-realization; and (3) problematic fixing of power as resolvable by means of an ethics of gift.

Normalization of suffering

While messianic sensibilities are present during the period of slavery, the end of slavery as a formal system would serve to make explicit and visible some of the underlying assumptions of early African American Christology, particularly in terms of a reconfiguration of the messiah figure. To the extent redemptive suffering argumentation undergirds much of African American social justice rhetoric as opposition to white supremacy, messianic formulations of African

American identity are to be expected. Based on this model, African Americans have at times posited the African American community as a transfiguration of Christ—the "one" whose suffering and pain will redeem the nation.[32] By so doing, African American Christology projects a matrix of life that is fixed and reified—without explanation or engagement that does not center on human suffering as the basic structuring of existence. That is to say the perpetuation of the Christ Event mythology as the primary language of African American Christian engagement with the world requires the presence of suffering as both the marker of need and the mechanism of transformation.

The most notable marker of this perspective is the notion of redemptive suffering whereby African Americans understand the resolution of moral evil to take place through suffering: "no cross, no crown," or some version thereof. What this prevents is creative engagement with the world that does not presuppose suffering—does not use relationship to suffering as the measure of both pain and progress. Instead, suffering becomes already and always.

African Americans are positioned to serve as the scapegoat, the means by which transformation takes place. Their bodies become the necessary substitute to the extent they understand their relationship to the world (and God) through transfigurations of Christ. Further reenforced by the normalization of human suffering by means of Christology is the assumption that redemption comes by means of an external mechanism—an exchange by which particular bodies accept stigma in order to open space for large-scale social transformation. Or, drawing on Rene Girard, one might understand this depiction of blackness as constitutive of Christ entails a type of sacrifice concerned with the production of harmony.[33] It signifies the violence of white supremacy through a willingness to take on a prime example of violence—Jesus Christ—absorbed.

There is something of this meaning in theologian Delores Williams understanding of the surrogate, but rather than seeking to reject this role as she hopes to do theologically many African American Christians have embraced it as a means of communal and social restoration. Sacrifice centers the transfiguration.[34] In other words, "We inherit the tradition of Christian morality which makes self-renunciation the condition for salvation. To know oneself was paradoxically the way to self-renunciation."[35] The stigma of blackness within the context of a discourse of whiteness is altered through a transfiguration of Christ whereby blackness is given Christological and by extension anthropological merit on the highest epistemological and ontological levels. Yet, this move simply reenforces another stigma—the African American (collective) Christ figure as stigmatized figure whose suffering is redemptive.[36] A social stigma becomes a theologically contrived and ethically enacted stigma—undergirding a metalanguage and conceptual paradigm of race as already and always a meaningful difference. It gives the stigma great importance, cosmic importance within teleology of human redemption. Of limited consequences is whether or not all recognize this positioning of the stigmatized. The demands of the larger society—as presented in/through a discourse of whiteness as normative—can be denied without significant impact as those claiming the stigma of the blackened Christ are "insulated by [their] alienation, protected by identity beliefs of [their] own, [they feel that they are] full-fledged normal . . . [they bear] a stigma but [do] not seem to be impressed or repentant about doing so."[37] In fact, the stigma becomes the marker of their importance, their contribution to the advancement of the moral and ethical nature of life. The stigma—blackness over against whiteness—becomes a marker of excellence, or deep meaning in that categorical racism[38] is addressed through the transfiguration of a few vis-à-vis altered Christ image and Christ-like postures toward the world (e.g., redemptive suffering).

Shadow presence of whiteness

Scapegoats are necessary, and whiteness suggests the "stain" of blackness as the proper markings of the sociopolitical, economic, and cultural scapegoat for the United States. Stigma defines the visual and discursive articulation of this marking in certain ways.

Even the blackening of Christ as briefly presented above serves to reenforce the centrality of whiteness, although as a negative to be addressed. Either way—as conceptual paradigm to critique or as shadow presence to which blackness responds—whiteness remains central and continuing to connote power. In this way discourse on whiteness as salvific—the ontological and material link to the divine will—is short-circuited through theological manipulation of the very mechanisms used to safeguard white domination—systematic domination vis-à-vis group suffering of African Americans. This proposition bears significant difficulties in that suffering easily becomes the standard of black life—the inescapable measure of existence. In this way, discourse on African American communities' messianic role becomes a normative statement on the "natural" condition of life for African Americans.[39] African American Christology challenges the status of whiteness as conceptual paradigm, but it does so in a way that maintains the embedded integrity of racialized structuring of information and meaning. Whether in white or black, African American Christology continues to posit the significance of race formation as having "real" importance and meaning. And, to the extent this is the case, African American Christology in the form of "black" Jesus imagery reenforces whiteness in that blackness remains a response to, or a consequence of, whiteness. It is dependent on the "space" made available through the matrix of whiteness. A correction of whiteness through blackness continues the discourse of whiteness and maintains a sense of race-based self-awareness as normative. In either case, presentation of the African American continues to entail stigma.[40]

Some years ago theologian Victor Anderson provided a compelling explication and critique of this metasymbol of whiteness lurking behind racial discourse—particularly the ontological blackness that many theologies have used to describe both God and Christ. Through this projection of blackness as antiwhiteness, African American presentations and understandings of self are truncated. And what Ann Branaman says regarding Erving Goffman's theory of the self, such restrained understanding forces a defining of self "in congruence with the statutes, roles, and relationships they are accorded by the social order."[41] In this instance, this involves a blackness created by reaction against a whitened embodiment of *imago Dei*. Such a move seems to suggest an authentic person can be transfigured through attention to the compromise of time and space offered by personification of the Christ account. But even this draws one back to the significance of whiteness in that the meaning and importance of the blackness of Christ—the rejection of whiteness as having theological and ontological importance—depends on the perpetual target of whiteness. Hence, while the blackening of Christ might symbolically and ethically render African American Christ-like, the necessity of whiteness for this development renders whiteness God-like.[42] Put another way, "because black life is fundamentally determined by black suffering and resistance to whiteness (the power of nonbeing), black existence is without the possibility of transcendence from the blackness that whiteness created . . . existentially, the new black being remains bound by whiteness."[43]

Problematic fixing of power

Transfigurations of Christ through challenge to the whitening of Jesus Christ reframe the black body as sign or symbol altered by its ability to communicate or channel the will of God. By this move, African Americans attempt to use theological categories to visually alter their status over against the ramifications of whiteness as normative. This mistake, however, is the implied assumption that recasting of the black body vis-à-vis applied Christology effectively alters power and its impact—assuming this new articulation of the blackness on black bodies places African American Christians outside the "social fiction" of whiteness.[44] Even this Christ-like, black body, is a symbol of the social system—power continues to define and shape it. The difference here involves the manner in which this theological move entails the reconstitution of the socially constructed body—the new body of Christ as black—as Michel Foucault might suggest, is still observed and controlled, although the assumption is this new configuration of blackness exposes, challenges, and frees African Americans from this constraining influence.

The effort may be to transform the body so as to gain a measure of relief from the workings of whiteness as power discourse, but even this transformation maintains limitations, restrictions consistent with the discourse created by whiteness. The presentation of the African American is still monitored and arranged in light of whiteness in that it takes places within the context of social structures and practices once shaped by the nature and meaning of racial discourses. To the extent Christology anchors theological anthropology and ethics it seeks to address issues of domination and control by means of a passive act of surrogacy—marking out transformation as a process of moralized suffering. Transfigurations of Christ, then, seek to generate new schematics of life.

Connected to this is a flawed assumption: power is "held" by embodied bodies, and that power can be secured through actions that counter the dominant social motif. Instead, I find compelling Foucault's understanding of power as working in and through bodies, but not held by particular individuals or groups. So understood, the presentation of a messianic figure—even when "black"—allows for an illusion, a misunderstanding of power and its function that serves to reenforce the workings of power to control discourse and thereby life meaning. Furthermore, the basic meaning of the Christ Event suggests it is possible to view and work on problems of power (e.g., whiteness and limitation on life) from outside the structures of oppression and in awareness of the mechanisms of control. Christology also seems to suggest that power can be arranged and controlled through particular ethical acts. However, it is more likely that power is not so easily understood, does not relate to particular truths, and is present in and through this reconfiguration of Christ and Christology. In this regard, "human subjects and historical events are not firm and discrete (id)entities but are fragmented and changing sites across which the flows of power move."[45] This may involve a different "mapping" of the body through a Christological repositioning of *imago Dei*, but even this mapping bears the marks of a racial discourse that controls the nature and meaning of African Americans and their bodies. This theological turn is an "improvement" of the status and meaning of blackness, but even this involves reflection against whiteness. Yet, this altered Christology is still the "blackness that whiteness created" because it amounts to "racial apologetics" writ theologically.[46]

As I have argued elsewhere, fighting racism as a form of power relations does not entail fighting particular individuals or groups. Power is a series of relationships found in everything and through everything—making and informing bodies. Hence, an attack on white supremacy as expressed in relationship to particular groups does not end the problem when one consider the fluidity of power relationships and the knowledge connected to them as well as the manner in which these same power relationships flow from the "oppressed." Struggle, then, takes on connotations and possibilities less robust and "meaningful" as that posited by liberation theologies. Such theologies seek to detangle black bodies from the power dynamics of oppression, but perhaps if Foucault is correct, such thinking is to misunderstand the nature of power and knowledge, and to assume the body has a prehistory reality, and to think power does not flow through and by means of black bodies as well.[47]

Christology actually renders bodies docile—in line with the discourse of control and relationship generating the status quo—rather than encouraging the formation of embodied bodies that seek to expose the dynamics of power and control. The transfiguration of Christ within the context of African American struggle against white supremacy assumes a linear sense of progress, a certainty of transition in that action (the activities of Christ manifest in the workings of African Americans who are Christ-like) generates particular outcomes. That is to say this transfiguration of Christ suggests power is held and can be redirect based on the strength of moral and ethical positioning. Christology as an effort to rethink theological anthropology so as to counter the effects of whiteness and discourse of domination involves a reconstitution of black bodies on the level of discourse, the level of cultural construction.

Relatively untouched by this proposition, however, is the embodied body to the extent the transformative demands made by liberal theologies cannot be sustained through Christology and an accompanying ethics. Theology may map the body but not in a way that *isn't* compromised by an always and already arrangement of power relationships—despite what is theologically said about race as a mode of authority.[48] As I have noted elsewhere, liberal theologies, by highlighting the body as metaphor—as symbol of the meaning of blackness over against whiteness, are in fact offering a religious-theological etiology of white supremacy; but, they do not give sufficient attention to adequately addressing the experience of white supremacy and by extension the materiality of the body and the materiality of liberation.

Theological anthropology presupposed by the blackness of Christ (over against whiteness) involves a static sense of identity or meaning that limits African Americans, and downplays the significance of how their bodies occupy time and space. Christology actually looks beyond the body—sees the body but is only able to claim it as a matter of discourse—shifting signs and symbols articulated. The challenge to visual images of whiteness through an alternate Christology—or a blackening of transfigurations of Jesus Christ—may entail an effort on the part of some African Americans to constitute African Americans as subjects, but the end product is a theologized body, a discursive body—with little impact on the embodied body that remains restricted by social arrangements and political mechanisms of control.

Material bodies are born, live, grow old, and die. However, Christology is not concerned with the articulation of relationship to this embodied body, but rather seeks to focus on the culturally/theologically constructed body—the one that gives itself and in the process seeks to abandon our materiality, or our "finitude . . . our inescapable physical locatedness in time and space, in history and culture . . ." This materiality, which includes race and gender, cannot be escaped through Christology; it simply determines who African Americans are as the blackened Christ and who the blackened Christ is in light of whiteness.[49]

Change in plans: The life meaning and progress sought by African Americans and every other human community require people doing their best within the limits of their morality, ethics, and vision. In this, and in other, ways, Jesus does not matter—does not offer anything substantive to human striving.

8

Gathering the godless: Intentional "Communities" and ritualizing ordinary life

God and Jesus discussed in previous chapters provide some of the framing and grounding for theistic communities. This stems from the requirement those devoted to Jesus in/and God gather together. God, through Christ, is believed to be present during such gatherings, even when they are small in number: "For where two or three gather in my name, there I am with them."[1] The disciples gathered during Pentecost and, according to the story, good things occurred that resulted in the expansion of a Christian community beyond the boarders of its initial home.[2] Such attention to connection is not limited to Christians; others such as Buddhists and Hindus produce architecturally significant and aesthetically appealing spaces for the adherents to gather. The same is certainly the case for Muslims, whose mosques present the physical framing for devotion to the divine and recognition of human interaction.

Bringing together the like-minded is a significant consideration for theists, but they are not alone regarding recognition of the beneficial dynamics of relationship. Questions of gathering together are real for humanist as well, and in this chapter some attention is given to how humanists ritualize life within the context of community.

Contextual considerations

I understand the push among many humanists and atheists to center thought and activism around issues of separation of church and state as well as science education. Beyond the rock star status of certain iconic figures such as Richard Dawkins within humanism and atheism, it is assumed often that science is the best language for unpacking collective life and that churches—as a significant representation of the "religious"—have held undue sway over public (read political) thought and practice for far too long. So, advance science and detangle the connections between "religion" and the state. Through this process produce social arrangements premised on reason and all the good (assumed) generated through that structuring of collective life.[3]

I have covered much of this ground elsewhere in the volume, and my intent is not simply to rehearse it here. But for context, I restate my point that there is something to this logic in that it advances the benefits of critical thinking and works to ensure a democratic space for national exchange that is not restricted and truncated by theistically theological ideals and frameworks of meaning. Yet, there is a downside—a type of harm on the conceptual, and by extension, thought and praxis level. In a word, this focus on policy and science misses dimensions of our existential lives that are best captured by the poetic—by a vocabulary and grammar more creative and sensitive to the dynamics of the awe-inspiring relationships material life can entail.

I have hinted at this downside, as I perceive it, through my qualified framing of "religion" over against "theism." In a word, I think humanists and atheists suffer from a misnaming that does damage to the ability to live humanism. I mean to say, humanists and atheists often fail to make a distinction between theism and religion, although humanist and atheist rhetoric would suggest the former is the real target of disbelief.

The difference between theism and religion

My distinction between theism and religion is not simply wordplay; it is not a matter of semantics. There, I believe strongly, is a substantive distinction between the two. Theism, as humanists and atheists note, involves belief in something beyond human history—some type of Unity of meaning (e.g., God or gods) that informs, shapes, and directs the workings of the universe in general and human history in particular. They, theists that is, shape their conceptual relationship to life and the world in light of the dictates and obligations demanded by this Unity, and they do this in ways meant to suggest a link to a reality beyond the reach of human reason and science. Common examples of theism so defined would of course include Christianity, Islam, Buddhism (to some degree), Judaism, Voodoo, Santeria, and Hinduism. These and other traditions are targeted by humanists and atheists in a variety of ways—written literature, conversation, billboards, lawsuits, and so on.

Humanists and atheists rightly point out the manner in which so many of the theological sensibilities, ethics, and morals of theists push against reasonable inquiry, promote dehumanization of particular groups (e.g., gays and lesbians), and seek to shape public life around a truncated and doctrinally arranged set of rules and regulations. This, for example, is at times framed in terms of the assumption the United States is a Christian nation and should promote domestic and foreign policies and practices that highlight biblical pronouncements.[4]

Even, the argument goes, when these organizations venture into social transformation-minded activities, this work takes place in ways that are strangled by theological insights, that are limited, and that are framed in terms of an "in" group (i.e., believers") and an "out" group composed of all others. I note this elsewhere in the volume, and do so here to highlight the presence of a posture toward society that does not allow the best workings of democratic principles.[5]

Theism has its critics and, based on the history of various forms of theism, this is for solid reasons. However, too many humanist and atheist critiques lack a nuanced understanding of theory of religion—drawing from personal anecdotes and pedestrian assumptions rather than scholarship. This is odd considering the way in which these groups demand informed scientific conversation from theists. The evidence of this poor thinking includes the conflating of theism and religion, as if they are synonymous. Stemming from this logic is an assumption that there is a distinct category of orientation one might call "nonreligious."

Numerous books, articles, conferences, and the like point to a growing intellectual curiosity regarding what is referenced as "nonreligion" and as secularity.[6] However, from my intellectual vantage point, a push against traditional modalities of the "religious" in the form of atheism, humanism, and so on does not necessarily entail nonreligion. Much of what concerns scholars (e.g., sociologists) exploring what they label "nonreligion" or secularity involves qualitative considerations regarding shifting population from belief to disbelief, as well as structural and ideological markers of this shift. Quantitative studies also explore similar developments. Such studies—both quantitative and qualitative—give some attention to the manner in which this shift is expressed in the form of communal developments and ritualized processes. My concern in this chapter, however, is a bit different.

Demographic considerations are not addressed here, and communal activities noted, as by-product of these demographic shifts, are not my particular focus. Instead, I am interested in how nontheists (however they get to that position and despite their particular percentage of the population) ritualize and orchestrate community. That is to say, not why, but *how* do the godless gather? Some scholars suggest one reason for adherence to belief or disbelief involves perceived threat; yet, there is also something to the notion that not external threat (e.g., the influence of conservative religiosity on life choices such as pro-choice and gay rights) but internal need motivates the ritualization of life within community. This would mean an internal push for connection and ways to recognize the weight and significance of the metaphysical issues addressed within the context of human history and empirical experience.[7]

Again, theism and religion are not the same: all theisms are religion, but not all religion is theism.

This may come across as too fine a distinction for some; nonetheless, it is an important distinction in that it opens various possibilities to humanism not otherwise in place. For example, it detracts from the significance of humanists constantly describing themselves in opposition to the "religious." By making this adjustment, humanists are able to devote more time and energy to productive ventures as opposed to a perpetual self-understanding premised on negation: "we aren't religious."

There is no reason to believe use of the terms "religion" or "religious" requires one set of signs, symbols, and practices. No, the language of religion is more flexible, and more fluid-like than that, despite what fundamentalists are wont to argue. Rather, to use the language of religion simply means to connote particular orientations that help humanists and atheists to wrestle with meaning and provide a framing and vocabulary for that wrestling. In a word, whether one is theistic or nontheistic in one's thinking and practices, there is a basic human need to render life meaningful. Theists do this through a turn to metaphysics guided by divine beings impinging upon the world, and nontheists do this by relying strictly on the abilities of the human animal.

Again, religion, I want to argue, should not be collapsed into theism. Religion is a "binding together"—an approach, or system, for attempting to make life meaningful. It is a framing of human experience so as to answer the large ontological and existential questions of our existence: who, what, when, where, and why are we? It is a way to theorize and a method for sifting through human experience in search of something that will render meaningful human encounters with the world. Religion is a framework for capturing elements of historically situated human experience and exploring them for what they say to and about these metaphysical questions.[8] It is a tool for confronting what appears absurd and meaningless. Religion so conceived is not *sui generis*. In fact, it has no substance, no essence, no internal "something." More to the point, *religion isn't a unique mode of experience—one that points (of necessity) beyond human reason and human history.*

When religion is thought of in this way—and this *is* a perfectly acceptable way of framing it—there is no need for it to be limited to theism and to theists.

Contrary to that limited ownership, religion is a human interpretive device that points back to us.[9]

Some might consider this akin to "religious atheism," the mode of philosophical and ethical questioning/answering proposed by figures such as Martin Heidegger and Friedrich Nietzsche as well as what some want to consider the stance of Albert Camus—someone who receives significant attention in this book.[10] For the first two at least, the atheistic stance is minimally aware of—if it does not in some ways lament—the absence or "death" of God.

This atheism recognizes the troubled nature of life. For it, there is present already and always a connection to death and limitation. But it looks for other foundations, other means by which to confront the void, hence rendering it a "religious" atheism to the extent it seeks foundations (although they are not to be found as theists find them). What I point to is simply another perspective, a variation on a theme, which is atheism and humanism entail a push for meaning; but for these two orientations there is no grand Unity that provides this meaning. Nonetheless, humans seek it, desire it, search for it, and develop structures by which to categorize what they do/do not find. To state the claim again, atheism and humanism structure particular approaches to the quest for meaning and therefore they can be understood as religious.

Community for humanists and atheists?

Mindful of my explanation above, terms such as "irreligious" or "irreligion," while meant to signify something of the distinction between theism and atheism, fail to connote the more accurate distinction. "Irreligion" speaks to the doubt, the "secularity" of the age—the displacement of theology and the deep suspicion regarding metaphysics as theistically contrived. At least one early advocate of sociological analysis of irreligion defined it as "those beliefs and actions, which are expressive of attitudes of hostility or indifference toward the prevailing religion, together with indications of the rejection of its demands."[11] Unfortunately, such an understanding fails to account sufficiently for the ongoing ritualization of life, the continued poetic quality of our collective dealings that is captured by the language of the "religious."

Even efforts to argue that the religion-irreligious idea represents a spectrum of opinion fall short of what I have in mind.[12] To extend the argument, while some argue particular movements provide ways of thinking and doing that are consistent with irreligion, I would argue Ethical Culture, UUA, for example, are not irreligious in orientation.

True, both Ethical Culture and the UUA want social arrangements without the encumbering of superstition and theological dogma. Still, this does not necessarily entail a disregard for the ritualization of life that allows for some mystery—albeit a mystery grounded in the wonder of human, historical bound, togetherness.[13] Instead, they transcend the theological limitations of theism by highlighting the ethical and moral dimensions of human obligation. And, rather than linking these moral and ethical obligations to any particular theistic sensibility, they tie them to human agency and obligation. That is to say, while *neither* of these two—Ethical Culture and Unitarian Universalism— are necessarily theistic (although some UU congregations are and some of its leadership certainly pushes for Christianization), they are religious as I have defined religion.

Furthermore, not all UUs claim to be religious. The vocal atheists and "secular" humanists within the Association certainly do not; but, even they gather within churches, perform rituals that resemble theologically gutted Christian practices, and sit alongside those who do understand themselves as religious, but perhaps not theists. This segment of the UUA population may lament some of the more theistic elements of church services, but they attend. They complain from within the four walls of the church. Ethical Culture, again, has been described as a religion of ethics—no gods but plenty of advocacy for good conduct. All this is to suggest there is flexibility in use and meaning of the term "religion" already present within organizations that are at the least humanism friendly. This alone should be enough to encourage rethinking the utility and impact of this conceptual paradigm—religion.

There are numerous benefits to this discussion regarding the nature and meaning of religion. I address only one here, and it has to do with religion's framing of struggle for community, for processes (and a language) for ritualizing life within nontheistic circles of existence. This is what I mean: it is often the case that humanists and atheists—those who have thrown out both theism and religion—have a difficult time forging mechanisms for doing more than critiquing the "religious" and advancing a science agenda. The "soft" side of life—the circumstances of our living such as the birth of a child, the loss of a loved one, the joy of ritualizing our movement through time and space—is more difficult for them to address with recognizable compassion.

All too often ritual is perceived as a bad word—"shit," "fuck," and "damn" receiving fewer negative reactions than "ritual" when spoken in some humanist circles. This reaction stems from the assumption talk of ritual means the infiltration of religion into humanism and atheism. Contamination! At times, humanists and atheists who are open to ritual are understood as "accommodationistic," and the mocking can go beyond labeling. Still, *human*ists—as the name makes clear—and atheists do recognize the significance of our humanity as the "stuff" out of which we move through the world.

The challenge when faced with issues of communal interaction is to recognize the dimensions of that humanity that require care and comfort beyond legal challenges to theistic interventions into public and private life. In too many instances, the motivation is to build humanism over against nurturing humanists. The two might overlap at points, but they are not identical. I hope what I perceive as an increase in energetic (or at least frequent) exchange regarding humanist communities of all sorts suggests recognition of this distinction and an increased concern with the latter (i.e., care and comfort). If I am correct, general and academic conversation concerning the secularization of societies—with figures in the United States pointing to particular European examples—does not erode the reality of continued human effort toward concern with life meaning as well as efforts to speak to the collective nature of this desire for meaning within the context of community (both virtual and localized).[14]

Celebration of secularization has not constituted the demise of theistically expressed religion. This mode of religion and its institutions/content has shifted and changed, with only the most inflexible dying off. By inflexibility I do not mean evangelical or conservative. Instead I mean organizationally rigid, with firm modes of proselytizing, and the inability to adapt to new strategies and styles of expression. There is reason to take note of this evolution of religiosity: The preferences of the "Nones," and one could highlight the Millennials within that grouping, point to a spread of sensibilities that often privilege a sense of connectedness to something greater than the individual but without preoccupation with traditional explanations of or framings for this sense that entail God or gods.

Many of these "Nones"—those who claim no particular religious affiliation—name their orientation through the language of spirituality; others use more fluid notions of the religious, while still others push in the direction of nontheistic humanism and atheism. Some go so far as to blend these various categories—atheism, spirituality, and religious—in unique ways. Furthermore, for a noteworthy grouping of these "Nones" there is concern with forging community that entails time and spaces set aside and set apart for the rituals of togetherness as ways to mourn loss, celebrate well-being, and offer some of the other amenities that were traditionally associated with theistic organizations. In short, they suggest an alternate cartography of the religious.

The human need for connection, for relationships that acknowledge the "stuff" of human existence—the joys, sorrows, pains, and so on—remains intact for these folks. But theistic language and practices are inadequate for the task of responding to this stuff of life. These persons, and in this volume the concern is with the humanists in groups, have not given up religion per se but instead they have rejected particular framings of the religious in the form of traditional theistic organizations and their theological renditions of meaning.

Of continuing significance for these humanists (based on attention to the implications of what scholars like Kate Hunt have documented through quantitative study) are spaces of reflection and gathering, dedicated locations for conscious manipulation of time and space so as to forge connections with others in relationship and in recognition of a shared desire for the expression of human purpose.[15] Ethical Culture and the UUA have perceived themselves as having the capacity to fill this need for relationship and ritualization of the ordinary.

If nothing else, the fact that they have not closed their doors, have not sought affiliation with other "liberal religion" organizations, or even radically changed their "style" of presentation suggests at least some relevance for these two religious organizations. In fact, new branding efforts speak to an assumption the UUA, for instance, has something to offer a wider range of persons than currently represented in their numbers. From a new logo, to alternate ways of speaking about what the organization offers, the UUA is working to help the overarching Association and the local congregations develop better ways of speaking about Unitarian Universalism in light of current sociocultural dynamics informing life in the United States. Of course, the goal, while only addressed dimly, is to expand the brand and gain new members for an Association in danger of numerical collapse. "This is the beginning," the UUA statement on branding indicates, "of a long transformative journey to tell the story of us and inspire individuals to join that journey."[16] As a member of the UUA, I applaud the effort to reenvision and in that way to assess the organization's place within the marketplace of human need. But is a fundamental element overlooked?

Will the aesthetic, the cartography of Sunday, the ritualization of the ordinary on the weekend, speak to this new branding? Will there be continued dissonance between theological self-understanding and ritualization of that understanding? In light of its theological formulations, why ever call these gatherings "worship," or the site of gathering a "church"? In a word, the theology and the Sunday ritualization entail a tension that is not necessarily productive. It is true the UUA contains wide-ranging theological perspectives and stances. (The UUA expresses this theological flexibility through the slogan, "deeds, not creeds.") Yet, these theological differences do not generate significantly different styles of gathering.

As already noted, Ethical Culture is often described as the "religion of ethics." Underlying this label is a sense the proper function of the religious—the mega-framing of life—is lodged in ethics rather than doctrinal creeds and theological pronouncements. While seeing its posture toward religion as differing from traditional theism, so much of the structuring of shared time within Ethical Culture suggest the lingering shadow of theistic worship—the architecture of the space, the manner in which time is marked out, the lecture (often very sermonic), and so on points to a religion of ethics ritually expressed through traditional theistic aesthetics.

The framing of the Sunday gathering resembles the shell of theistic worship, with the substance simply removed. Little, I would argue, about the central activities of a Sunday in the UUA or Ethical Culture speaks in substantive ways to a radically different theological posture. And this is the case whether one is visiting a decidedly atheistic congregation or a theistic congregation. If one were to block one's ears and avoid hearing the proceedings, the arrangement of bodies, the gestures, the practices, and the activities would be difficult to distinguish based on theological rationale. Sunday gatherings entail dissonance—a disconnect between what is perceived as alternate theological and philosophical claims and what is reminiscent of traditional Sunday "worship."[17]

New gatherings of the godless—Sunday assemblies

Perhaps the UUA and Ethical Culture, as two of the long-standing locations for godless gatherings, might shift locations? They might mark out space aesthetically, geographically, and symbolically only by the figures present—the human bodies gathered? Perhaps humanists might remove the dedicated space of the "church" structure as the primary marker of the right to gather?

Or, perhaps the UUA and Ethical Culture will remain as they are, for as long as they can maintain the limited memberships they have in place. What I have said is not intended as dismissive or a cold and harsh statement. Rather, it is simply descriptive of current conditions. One can read the signs: there is a lack of substantial growth for these two organizations; and, this is in direct opposition to the development of alternate and more organic methods of ritualizing life.

Some benefit of gathering might take place within the context of humanist and atheist annual conferences, for instance. And, one might recognize these as providing something similar to the community offered by Sunday Assemblies, etc. However, there are differences. For example, those conferences do not work based on a shared assumption that ritualization of life is vital—no necessarily shared communal ethos. They are not localized and regularized as these assemblies and humanist communities are "fixed."

One might think of these new organizations as a ritual web, with numerous points of contact, with each segment lending strength to the overall structure. Some elements of these new gatherings signify much of what has constituted godless worship by exaggerating certain dimensions of togetherness and downplaying some of the typical elements of worship (think UU and Ethical Culture approaches) that mark off individuals and downplay engagement through and with the body. Perhaps most prominent among these efforts is the Sunday Assembly model, which takes as its mission to "live better, help often, and wonder more."[18] Sunday Assembly brings the ordinary into ritualization through, for instance, the playing of games, telling of jokes, and so on. I believe this appreciation for the significance and wonder of the everyday is what is meant when The Sunday Assembly leadership says its meetings seek to "inject a touch of transcendence into the everyday."[19] This goal is constituted along the following lines. It:

1. Is 100 percent celebration of life. We are born from nothing and go to nothing. Let us enjoy it together.
2. Has no doctrine. We have no set texts so we can make use of wisdom from all sources.
3. Has no deity. We do not do supernatural but we also will not tell you you are wrong if you do.
4. Is radically inclusive. Everyone is welcome, regardless of their beliefs—this is a place of love that is open and accepting.
5. Is free to attend, not-for-profit and volunteer run. We ask for donations to cover our costs and support our community work.
6. Has a community mission. Through Action Heroes (you!), we will be a force for good.
7. Is independent. We do not accept sponsorship or promote outside businesses, organizations, or service.
8. Is here to stay. With your involvement, The Sunday Assembly will make the world a better place.

And, then, the leadership concludes by saying:

9. We will not tell you how to live, but will try to help you do it as well as you can.
10. And remember point 1 . . . The Sunday Assembly is a celebration of the one life we know we have.[20]

Much of The Sunday Assembly philosophy echoes the liberal stance of the UUA or Ethical Culture, but it has captured the imagination and involvement of Millennials in a way the former two have not—with local Assemblies in the United Kingdom, the United States, and Australia. Being nice, positive, and committed to well-being is not unique to The Sunday Assembly; many advocates of the UUA and of Ethical Culture would argue the same as the basic posture of their organizations.

The Sunday Assembly model appears to replace spirituality in a traditional sense with an effort to enliven embodied enjoyment of life. Still, The Sunday Assembly's DNA is the traditional church model. "The Sunday Assembly," we are told, "started on a car journey to Bath when two comedians, Sanderson Jones and Pippa Evans, realized that they wanted to do something that had all the best bits of church, but without the religion, and awesome pop songs."[21] In fact, it has been described as "part atheist church, part foot-stomping show, and 100 percent celebration of life."[22] Or, as Sanderson Jones remarks, it is something along the lines of "Pentecostalism for the godless."[23] The idea is for The Sunday Assembly to take on the full range of a church's tasks. "We have always said that Sunday Assembly is a phased growth into a full church life structure," Jones has said, and continues, "At Sunday Assembly London we are going to try to go weekly in 2014, and we are adding the services that you get at church. Pastoral care will first come in the form of small groups, with more serious problems being passed on to relevant service providers. However, we want to take care of the whole person."[24] Both virtually and physically present, The Sunday Assembly might just qualify as a movement that is exposing the softer dimensions of humanist identity.

The Sunday Assembly project began on January 6, 2013 and has grown since this initial meeting.[25] The leadership wants "a godless congregation in every town, city and village that wants one."[26] And, they have made it fairly easy for interested parties to join in and implement The Sunday Assembly model where they live. Yet, will the decidedly church-based aesthetic of The Sunday Assembly fulfill Millennials' wants and desires long term? I ask particularly in light of the tendency of Millennials to express, "boredom with the traditions in which they were raised. They've graduated, matured out of the need for regular reinforcement of the ethical teachings of the church"?[27] And, do they need to have their experience of togetherness, of communal engagement, take the shape of a church service? Even if church is simply a placeholder, a metaphor, does it have sustainability?

The Sunday Assembly has its critics, who question (with varying degrees of strength) the

1. Intent of the founders—self-promotion, or genuine concern?
2. Tenacious promotion of fun over against more "substantive" issues.

3   Turn to Christian vocabulary (e.g., church and congregation) to describe godless gatherings.

4   Utilization of structures for housing these gatherings that draw explicitly from theism—for example, church worship.

5   Lack of strong commitment to atheism or humanism as *the* philosophical stance of the assemblies.

Despite the critique, there is growth—undeniable interests on the part of many that keep the founders on the road, opening new assemblies.

Still, this is not the only model. Not all efforts to forge godless community embrace explicitly a church-based model, nor do all the architects of these efforts come to this work without ministerial sensibilities. Some former ministers are moving in this direction—repurposing their ministerial sensibilities to meet the needs of nontheists. What I have in mind and what I am interested in exploring more closely in this chapter are humanist communities such as Houston Oasis, in Houston, Texas.[28] Mike Aus, a former Christian minister, is its founder and current executive director.[29]

Humanists gatherings—The case of Houston Oasis

Currently located roughly 20–30 minutes from downtown, Houston Oasis developed a few years ago in response to a call for a space and time for nontheists to gather and celebrate life. In using the term "oasis," the community meant to distinguish itself from churches—both theistic and atheistic. Instead, it is "a community that meets regularly to create a place for freethinkers to celebrate the human experience. Each week we gather to discuss real-world principles based on reason, not tradition, which are supported by evidence, not scripture or revelation."[30] Its self-understanding resembles The Sunday Assembly's concern with human well-being, but its core values are more easily identifiable with humanist principles espoused by organizations such as American Humanist Association. Albeit decidedly humanistic, the turn to ethics is reminiscent of The Sunday Assembly's principles, while the posture of "fun" (i.e., comic entertainment) and amusement that undergird assemblies is not present in the same, explicit manner. One might expect this difference in light of the founders—The Sunday Assembly, comics and Oasis, a former minister. Mindful of this, the latter, Oasis, highlights the following values:

1. People are more important than beliefs;
2. Only human hands can solve human problems;
3. Reality is known through reason, not revelation;
4. Meaning comes from making a difference;
5. Labels are unimportant;
6. Everyone should be accepted wherever they are as long as they are accepting in turn.[31]

All the above is meant to provide the energy and organizational system necessary for people to center and make a difference. "The community comes together," the website says, "to enjoy coffee, live music, and to learn something new about the world, to draw strength from the power of human community, and to engage in service projects for the betterment of the human condition."[32]

Houston Oasis's current location resembles the typical office park building, but that aesthetic stops at the door. Smiling faces, outreached hands, and hearty "welcomes!" meet visitors and regulars as they enter the space. Moving down a short hallway with rooms housing, I assume, a variety of activities during the week, it does not take long to find the space that will house the weekly Houston Oasis gathering—typical room, florescent lights, a drop ceiling, chairs arranged with a lectern and table at the center.

There is a table to one side—the right as one enters the room—with nametags already printed and in plastic cases attached to a collar or sleeve for regulars, empty nametags and a pen for visitors and CDs for sale by the visiting musician.

In front, to the left, is a table with sound equipment and behind it, a screen announcing the title of the main lecture as well as the name of the lecturer. To the right of that screen is a board with some information like the location for lunch after the meeting, and attached to the wall on the right of that board is a sign listing the mission of Houston Oasis.

If one follows that wall moving right, one approaches a table with coffee, cups, and snacks. On each seat is a half-page sheet asking for information such as name, zip code, gender, occupation, etc. It is the type of guest information most churches would also find useful. At Houston Oasis, the top of the form says, "Thanks for joining us. We'd like to know more about you!" And this "knowing more" is to allow Houston Oasis to meet the needs of those gathered, to make certain its activities are consistent with what people want. Related to this, the last piece of information requested involves: "Volunteerism, outreach, or community service recommendations."

Dispersed throughout the room is a friendly crowd engaged in small talk, laughing—dressed in everything from sundresses, jackets, and slacks, to jeans and t-shirts. Clearly there is no dress code. The crowd, while primarily white American, cuts across age groups and economic groups (so it appears), and there are a few who would be called racial "minorities."

The scene is something of what one would expect before the start of a church service, one of the nondenominational and relatively youthful churches. This greeting of regulars and introductions to visitors over coffee and snacks continued, until a young man called the group to order. There is no bulletin outlining what will take place during the roughly 90-minute "meeting," but the regulars seemed to know and moved effortlessly through the time—taking in each moment with a type of verve I am not used to encountering in most humanist gatherings.

The young man who called the meeting to order then made a few announcements that met with some conversation. People seem free to speak out at any point. Black churches have something known as "call and response" during which members of the congregation will greet words from the minister with comments—"amen," "preach," and so on. But this was a bit different—even during the formal presentation. What took place at Oasis involved something more along the lines of a "kitchen table" conversation with its free-for-all quality.

Then, after the announcements and quick exchanges generated in response to them, there were a couple of musical selections from a guest musician; each song had humanists sensibilities highlighted: the beauty of relationship, accountability, and responsibility, in short—the celebration and ritualizing of life. After those songs—energetically applauded by the audience—the same young man reminded those gathered that members are free to share and that there are a few Sundays still in need of a speaker. After one person volunteered to give a presentation during one of the available Sundays, the young man continued by bringing to the front the person scheduled to provide casual reflection—thoughts that point to a practical lesson on how to live as a humanist.

In the reflection given there was some subtle critique of the "religious." Even those gathered in opposition to what some atheists and humanists would consider a negative—an effort to mimic theistic ritualization—could not help but lump theism and religion together. But here it seemed to be done without the same venom often found in such conversations. This, perhaps, is because the fundamental goal for Houston Oasis is to develop ways of interacting with the "religious" as opposed to simply bashing them.

The man's reflection lasting only few minutes was interactive, and it was followed by a 10-minute coffee break during which conversation continued and visitors were greeted and encouraged to "feel at home." For churchgoers this might resemble (san coffee and snacks) passing the peace or moments of welcome. The coffee break was followed by the "joke of the week" offered by a member of the group, and it was meet with an energetic response.

Following the joke, there was a song, and then the young man who seemed to be leader for the gathering on that particular Sunday introduced the speaker, who gave a 30–40-minute lecture—again a bit interactive. Lectures take place at every humanist and atheist gathering I have ever attending, but there is an "ease" at Oasis, which suggests this lecture is part of a community conversation, a secular moment of mutuality and sharing that prompts response—not quite black church "call and response," but engagement and appreciation expressed.

A brief "Q&A followed the lecture" and then additional announcements related to Houston Oasis community service projects. There was an offering—an invitation to give in support of the work Oasis is doing and in order to meet its basic expenses. Sacks were passed around for collecting contributions. This offering was followed by another song and informal conversation before the meeting leader, the young man, thanked everyone for coming and ended the gathering. Those interested were encouraged to make their way to the selected restaurant for the Houston Oasis lunch.

On "New" ritualized gatherings for the godless

While Oasis promotes itself as a community—a comforting space for human connection—and not as a church, little about the architecture of its meeting (e.g., songs, lecture [often with a sermonic tone meant to encourage adherence], and fellowship after the service) pushes clearly beyond a church structure of ritual activity. Whether claimed or not, the church-derived presentation of communal engagement on a Sunday still seems the default position. In this case, even resistance to it does not free from its basic framework.

Does *atheology* over against theistic theology mean humanist gatherings have to use the shell of theistic ritualization? Have theistic organizations promoted the only possible means of gathering in light of metaphysical concerns? Is there a way to link more organically the philosophical position of nontheists and a structure for gathering the godless that is not a shadow of theist congregational models of worship? That is to say, must fellowship always present itself through structures of embodied reflection and activity using the residue of theistic arrangements of celebration?

It is true these godless gatherings, even when resembling the structuring of theistic worship, point in an alternate metaphysical direction. Put differently, they do not gather for the benefit of some transcendent being or beings—for the recognition of something beyond human sensibilities and abilities. In this regard, these nontheistic activities are not meant to hide embodiment, or to project embodiment as a problem to solve. Rather, how bodies occupy time and space is given full meaning as the proper substance of human togetherness.[33] Embodied ritual for nontheists in this context points to connection with other fragile, mortal bodies—over against the body for the theist pointing to the need to transcend the body in order to gain true meaning and fellowship with the divine.

Still, the challenge is clear: how to ritualize these godless gatherings in ways that do not collapse into a structuring of time and activity drawn from theistic framing. For the former, nontheists, attention to the body is meant to give more vibrant possibility to life within the confines of the empirically understood world; but, for the latter, the theists, this attention to the body is meant as a chastisement. It is a marking of material existence as a barrier to real existence, and only rendering the body docile through worship can bring the human's true self closer to its creator. The former, nontheistic gathering is about the humans gathered and extends no further than the physical world. The latter, theistic gathering ultimately is about the relationship to a higher power of those gathered, and relationship between people in worship is meant to celebrate this shared devotion to something else.

Calls for community in various forms has involved at least two things: (1) systematic organizing of social activism and charity meant to demonstrate the humane nature of humanism as it reaches out to improve collective existence; and (2) ritualized gatherings meant to address the emotional, psychological, and communal dimensions of human personhood in relationship. As Harvard Humanist Chaplain Greg Epstein rightly notes, there is an increase in both local and virtual attention to gathering, to the forging of connections between humanists that are more social in nature—getting together for a drink, a community service project, a movie and discussion, and so on.[34] While concerned with the substance of such gatherings for what they say to and about human need for togetherness, Epstein and others continue assumptions regarding the nature of religion I questioned above. To be "good without God," as the title of his book proclaims, is not a denouncement of religion per se, but of a certain formulation of the religious as theistic in scope, orientation, and intent. That is to say, it is a certain response to metaphysical questions that dislodges the most valuable modalities of knowledge and being from empirical study and finding.

From my perspective there is less reason to parse out the nature of the religious with respect to the first of the two calls for community given above, but with the second it is a more substantial concern. What distinguishes these

Sunday Assemblies, Humanist Communities, Humanist churches, and so on? That is to say, what about the architecture—both physical and emotional—of these nontheistic gatherings speaks to a religious impulse over against what simply suggests a strategy for community activism, as Epstein seems to suggest at times?

Such questions do not distinguish religion from irreligion or nonreligion, but rather speak to the fluid nature of the religious and its ability to capture competing metaphysical sensibilities and ideologies. Is there something about these communities that is marked by the lingering shadow of theistic ritual cartographies of engagement and relationship? Are they, church "lite"? This is more than the notion of "cultural Christian" touted by some.[35] Instead, it is a systematic recognition that people—even humanists—need connections, desire a response to the "softer" dimensions of life in the world in ways that comfort when mourning, and allow celebration during those moments of joy and happiness. It is being together in ways that value the individual by placing the self within the context of other selves.

Gatherings so orchestrated are meant, in another sense, to expand what one can know about life through a process of exchange. This might be discussed in terms of participants feeling "energized," "connected," "appreciated," "balanced," "not alone," and so on. Humans are social animals who at times wrestle with the most traumatic dimension of our self-awareness through shared practices orchestrated within the context of the like-minded.

And now . . .

Even these new modes of community suggested by Houston Oasis and similar organizations bear the shadow of their theistic alternatives. Little about their structuring of time together, for instance, reflects adequately the metaphysical shifts humanism and atheism entail. Mindful of this, I propose a radical turn as a corrective: get rid of the dedicated Sunday meeting as the primary marker of communal reflection and ritualization of the ordinary. This is not to suggest the Sunday gathering should go away completely, but instead its symbolic/ritual importance is decreased so as to better represent the humanist's commitment to the ordinary, empirical arrangements of life as having, shall I say, deep meaning each day of the week.

So, this being the case, why set aside Sunday at all, as if that gathering of the like-minded is more ritually significant than the gathering of the like-minded at any other point? Doesn't the Sunday get-together maintain the significance of that particular day as if it marks off something "sacred" or represents a meaning not captured at any other point during the week? Of course, it is the case that the weekend might be easier for some because of work schedules; but what of the humanists who work on weekends or have other obligations capturing Sunday time? Might it be the case that evenings, any given evening, might provide the same set of dedicated and set-apart times for the ritualization of the ordinary?[36] Or, perhaps the particulars related to gathering might be dictated by the schedules and obligations of the like-minded involved?

My thinking out loud on this topic is not the last word, and having the last word is not the intent. Rather, I want to point out what I consider a flaw in strategy, a structural slipup based on familiarity that should be addressed. My goal is not to provide a new framework because such work needs to be local and organic, but rather to provide issues to consider. I offer conceptual considerations that might inform the development of possibilities that are new indeed and tailored to the nature and meaning of humanism broadly conceived. So, do things different; produce modes of being together that are more organic to this particular cultural moment. And, doing this should entail consideration of at least the following:

1. A philosophy of life consistent and in line with the structuring of ritual gatherings;
2. A push beyond the theistically inspired sacralization of Sunday as set apart;
3. A centering of the human in *human*ism through attention to how bodies occupy time and space and the logic and mapping of togetherness;
4. A consideration of spaces for gathering that reflect humanism's critique of institutionalized theism and that advance its deep regard for the wonder of the physical world;
5. A recognition of the centrality of a poetic posture toward these gatherings;
6. Development of vocabulary and grammar for expressing the nature and meaning (as well as content) of these gatherings that better reflects humanistic wonder and reverence for life, that expresses humanistic metaphysics;
7. Determination of intended audience(s);
8. Comfort with multiple approaches to the significance of gathering rather than assuming this new structuring of the celebrated moment is *the* humanist arrangement;

9 Embrace a range of ritual items that mark organic connection to a humanist view on the interconnectedness of life and the significance of the material, natural world;

10 Make sure to connect these gatherings to the humanist business of fostering healthy life options within a more just society;

11 Demonstrate the humanist linking of ethics and metaphysics through this gathering and the space for this gathering;

12 Be sensitive to technological advances and challenges—for example, shifting distinction between physical and virtual community;

13 Be suspicious of "tradition" as a rationale for stagnation;

14 Address the issue of diversity without reducing difference to a problem;

15 Foster diversity as intrinsic to the nature and meaning of communal gathering;

16 Reflect local sensibilities and environment; and

17 Be prepared to change.

While I have questions about this arrangement, Sunday could continue as the central element of that web structure. But it would no longer entail the same nod to traditional churches, nor homage to the conference presentation format. Instead, the aesthetic would privilege the fact that the Sunday gathering is a period of reporting back—an opportunity to share the outgrowth of humanistic sensibilities in practice and feedback meant to foster greater impact for such activities. During the rest of the week, segments of the community might gather related to particular projects or to address life episodes—deaths, births, etc. The objective embedded in the above is to decenter Sunday as it has been understood by theists and certain religious humanists, and to highlight the deep significance of everyday, the everyday or ordinary, as the location for significant humanist activity. Sunday, rather than a time still tied to a sense of the "sacred" is now a point for reporting back—for noting what it has meant to be a humanist during the course of the week. And, the rest of the week involves the doing of humanism—and this would include moments to address the joys and sorrows of our physical existence.

The significance given to humanity, the value placed on life within the existential contexts of human history without appeal to transcendence, invests with deep meaning what theists might consider mundane and nonconsequential (in an ultimate sense) activities such as eating a meal with loved ones. They, in a sense, become sacramental activities of a sort—activities of a celebratory nature. Such is a perspective on the sacramental nature of "ordinary" life, the depth of meaning found in the uneventful events of life. In this respect, the very acts of living within the context of community involve sacraments of sorts, rituals (e.g., repeated activities) of the ordinary.[37]

SECTION THREE

Cultural production

Humans construct and live within cultural worlds. Within these frameworks we develop the tools necessary to describe and discuss our encounter with each other as well as our relationship to/with the world.

Although humanists are aware of culture and surely engage with cultural developments, I suggest humanists have missed an important opportunity by not taking seriously some of the more marginal modes of cultural expression. I have in mind hip-hop culture. In two of the chapters in the third and last section of this book, I explore the way in which hip-hop culture's development, growth, and global reach should be of interest to humanist organizations concerned with experiencing similar growth and reach. That is to say, there are important lessons offered by hip-hop culture concerning branding, language development, outreach, and so on. In addition, I use hip-hop (and the thought of Albert Camus) to wrestle with the nature and meaning of the culture of death. Finally, the third chapter examines the cultural tool of language—signs and symbols—appropriate for describing and participating in public life.

The goal of these three chapters is to assert the need for humanists to think broadly regarding culture and cultural production, as well as for humanists to wrestle with what humanism might offer people seeking to negotiate their way through significant issues such as the end of life. In short, I seek to present humanism's impact on culture/cultural production and the latter's impact on humanism.

9

Learning to be cool, or making due with what we do

The second section of the volume ended with a chapter discussing humanist effort to ritualize life, to forge godless gatherings by means of which humanists are able to work through joy, pain, etc. Mindful of need for humanists to express themselves and to value relationships noted in that piece, this chapter raises a question: Is victory over the doctrine of God all nontheistic humanists desire? Is this victory even the best symbol of humanist self-understanding?[1] (We humanists and atheists tend to be as focused on God as theists!) If so, it is a somewhat empty victory, and at its worst is it reminiscent of the posture of some evangelical theists?

I would hope humanism involves more than destruction of a symbol. But having more requires steps beyond the quick conclusion that theists are delusional.

This may sound a bit "preachy," and it might just be, but humanists need to move on and tackle new issues. Again, theism might get modified; yet, it is not going away. Mindful of this, the struggle to end religion in the form of theism is something of a quixotic quest. Don't we humanists, have more pressing concerns? Shouldn't we, anyway?

Moving beyond this particular philosophical itch involves getting over what philosopher William Jones has labeled a "theoretical atheism" (easily altered to include a "theoretical" humanism) marked by preoccupation with rejecting the existence of God. This "atheism of the mind" (or humanism of the mind for that matter) is focused on belief and unbelief, on breaking the back of a delusion while enhancing an appreciation for science as the marker of our better selves.[2] But there is another strand, one Jones labels practical or functional. This productive atheism (or humanism, I would argue) involves more than the discrediting or lampooning of the practices of theistic faith communities. Atheism (and all those who reject notions of the Divine) is all too often, yet not always, presented as a simple negation of things religious, the "a-" meaning, simply, "not." Instead, atheists (and those who hold to naturalistic philosophies of life) must more carefully present a system of ethics meant to enhance quality of life. This must include both scientific advancement and rigorous struggle against irrational modes of destruction such as racism, sexism, and homophobia. What is necessary is the application of practices that speak clearly to concern for life within the context of a fragile environment.

To the extent it is possible (and many will reject this suggestion), attention should be given to a search for common ethical ground that brackets the harsher presentations of both theistic and humanistic/atheistic views. I am not asking for a "can't we all get along" rejection of debate and a suspension of aggressive wrestling over ideas. It is important to challenge beliefs as a way of safeguarding human accountability and integrity, but there must also be a push for more than destruction of all markers of theistic commitment.

The "godless" should continue to interrogate and critique theistic orientations, and adherents of theistic positions should continue to challenge humanists/atheists, lest the godless collapse into a fundamentalist atheism. If not, careful and self-critical attention paid to science by some atheists, for instance, could easily become scientism—a faith of its own.

The persistence of faith

I cannot say this often enough; history shows reason may alter the posture of faith-based communities, may force them to shift their language, and limit their size and their sociopolitical reach, but it will not destroy faith. The very definition of faith should make this apparent. According to scripture, it is "substance of things hoped for and the evidence of things not seen."[3] Humanists and atheists miscalculate the core significance of theism if they assume it is about doctrine and creeds, ritual forms, and physical structures. These things are attacked regularly. Yet this strategy of attack means little when theism, at its core, is about the making of meaning and the establishment of stories and practices related to how and why we occupy time and space. Ritual, doctrines, sacred texts, and so on are only cultural manifestations of this deeper meaning. These rituals and doctrines are secondary, not primary: They are modified, they shift, and they change to fit the particular historical-cultural context. Attacks on theism's theological or ritual shortcomings, while correct in some regards, will not end theism.

Theism and atheism/humanism will persist, and any real gain made toward healthy existence for our world must involve collaboration (not assimilation) and partnerships between moderates within both groups. This is not denial of difference and does not require rejection of one's chosen orientation. Rather it involves recognition that a mature approach to life rejects fundamentalism of any kind, and demands complex relationships of shared ethical commitment even when those relationships are burdened with tension.

To recap . . . and move on

To recap, I am a nontheistic humanist, and I am one who believes theism does more harm than good. It provides cosmic justification for all sorts of trauma and damage; it devalues human bodies and places bizarre restrictions on quality and content of life. Nontheists like me understand our work as, at least in part, addressing the stuff of theism that does harm to collective, public life.

Still, despite what I have said above, many of my atheist and humanist friends and acquaintances go the extra mile, believing that theism can and will be destroyed, that we are in the midst of a growing secularity. No longer content to be in the shadows, this group's effort to dismantle theism involves a blend of mockery and deep critique. Billboards, rallies, biting commentary—all this is meant to deconstruct the cultural worlds framing sacred texts and ideas, and to do deep damage to the stronghold theism has on life in the United States. I am in favor of billboards, as well as other organized effort to advance progressive values and life-affirming ethics. Why should theists alone be allowed to present their ideas in grand ways? The anger coming from theists when confronted with the absurdity behind some of their own faith commitments should not silence nontheists, and it does not require special handling by public figures.

Let theists be angry—it is an opportunity for conversation, for engagement.

While I do agree on the need for nontheists to be vocal and explicit in their critique and in the presentation of their views, I do not see that this type of activism will result in the demise, the final destruction of churches, and other traditional theistic institutions. I do not see that happening, and I am not sure it is even necessary.

Nontheists are due for a bit of introspection, for an honest assessment of atheist and humanist missions and objectives: What is the basic concern—the destruction of theism? Or, more specifically, the destruction of the poor patterns of thinking, communication, and practice supported by theistic religion? Does the development of human societies that are reasonable and more progressive require the end of theism or simply the containment of its most harmful dimensions? It is the latter that matters most. If traditional forms of theism go away some despicable human practices will lose their cosmic rationale.

Traditional, theistic religious traditions do not fall prey easily to logic and reason. In fact, the extreme examples of fundamentalism and evangelical thinking find attacks from nontheists an indication of their spiritual prowess. Ritual and theological structures insulate them from attacks on their most fundamental beliefs and practices.

Fundamentalist theology—the type atheists and humanists most typically attack—actually feeds off resistance and intellectual critique; these traditions run contrary to reason and logic, and there is little hope this will change. This type of theologizing is a prophylactic against thinking: faith trumps reason in such cases in that reason is perceived to be the arrogance of humanity.

Pointing out the symbolic or metaphorical nature of theistic claims, as I have done at points in this book, is important as a way of mapping out the deeply human and cultural nature of theism; but, it will not do deep damage to the ways in which sacred texts and rituals are applied to human life. It is likely theistic religions will transform but remain. And the growth of secularism in certain places does little to convince me otherwise, not in light of the rapid spread of Pentecostalism in Brazil, Prosperity Gospel-styled ministries in Africa, and so on.

What to do, and how hip-hop might help

A word of advice to atheists and humanists: deconstruct theistic models of religion—and expose the illogic and destructive thought and practice by those that have done so much graphic damage to human existence—but do not be delusional concerning the outcomes of such effort. It might be cathartic for atheist and humanists to broadcast their disdain for religion, but it does little to shake the theistic world. Only those who already harbor doubts fall prey to such attacks.

So, my atheist and humanist colleagues should continue to put up billboards, hold public events, lobby, and do everything possible to enter into public conversation on religion. And there is benefit to this, but nontheists of all kinds will continue to struggle and work within an environment composed of competing claims. And, this geography of perspectives requires attention to how we present ourselves. If humanists and other nontheists are honest about it, there is no doubt but that public relations and "branding" have not been the strong suit of the godless "movement." Help is needed if perception of nontheists within the public imagination is to improve, and for assistance I suggest turning to hip-hop culture. An unlikely connection, I know, but as the rest of this chapter is meant to demonstrate, it is a productive connection.

PR and branding

Humanists have made their presence felt. Often the rhetoric is self-assured, and vividly displayed is their willingness to confront the theism bias embedded in the workings of the United States. Despite all this, humanist activities still appear entrenched in an apologetic mode—a significant expenditure of resources meant to say, "we are here and, by the way, we are good people." Even more aggressive forms of humanist engagement, those meant to challenge the religious and convert them through strong confrontation and mockery betray, from my perspective, the same apologetic tone. Neither what some derogatorily call a conformist approach (i.e., accommodationism) nor the more self-righteous confrontational approach provides a sufficiently constructive and robust depiction of what humanistic orientations promote. This type of posture toward humanist work does not allow for the accomplishment of our full agenda to diminish the theism-centered discourse (and structures of interaction) guiding so many dimensions of public life. For sure, this is because humanists are still playing by the rules offered by theists. That is to say, there is embedded in their approach an effort to get theists to appreciate (perhaps even like?) humanists. But why worry about that? Furthermore, is this type of regard even achievable?

It can still be problematic to embrace publicly humanism. Yet the typical approach to this situation does little to change this dilemma in that the humanist's marginality is embedded in the rhetoric of the nation—and has become tragically the grammar of the public sphere—guided by the temperament of the uninformed. Even if this were not the case, being liked has not done much to change the outlook for other marginalized groups. What it can produce is paternalism, patronizing attitudes that actually stymie advancement and inclusion. Perhaps the godless might aim to be disliked, but respected? Yet, what does being respected entail for them? What is the look, the texture, of this respect and what does securing and keeping it require?

Help from an unlikely source: Hip-hop

Needed at this point is more attention to the construction of an alternate grammar of life along with new modalities of ethical/moral insight and practice that speak to the benefits of humanistic thinking and doing. Humanists have demonstrated some creativity in generating this message, but still seem a bit stuck and in need of inspiration. Again, mindful of this, I want to propose a source of assistance worthy of consideration—hip-hop culture.

What I have in mind extends beyond an appreciation for the outstanding work of humanists hip-hop artists, and instead includes attention to the pedagogical possibilities offered by the larger cultural movement. So, no need to worry; I am not asking readers to turn baseball caps backward, or forget about their sensible shoes and conservative clothing choices. I am not calling on humanists to become hip-hop advocates or fans. Rather, I am suggesting that hip-hop culture provides a particularly compelling heuristic. My aim is to encourage recognition of hip-hop as an interpretive tool by means of which humanists might learn how to better do what they say humanism is all about—and to do so in ways that appreciate the creativity lodged in their relative marginality and despised status.

A link between humanism and hip-hop is not as absurd as one might initially think, not when one considers a common epistemological root marking much of the thinking undergirding both. That is to say, both humanistic sensibilities and hip-hop culture share a human-centered and earthy ontology, both stem (although there are nuances to this) from a similar perception of evidence-based free thought and a signifying of supernatural claims and transhistorical assertions. Furthermore, in US culture, both humanists and members of the hip-hop community are labeled marginal and problematic figures whose activities/beliefs fly in the face of normative moral and ethical structures of life.

I propose an embrace of this epistemological connection and attention to what can be learned from the successes (and failures) of hip-hop culture. While it has its problematic dimensions—elements of violence, homophobia, misguided materialism, and so on borrowed from the storehouse of American culture—there are ways in which this cultural force has offered important challenges to the "American way of life." It has outlived calls for its demise and pronouncements of its fad-like quality. Even those who fear or dislike hip-hop culture have been forced to recognize it and address life in this historical moment in light of it.

Lodged within the decaying infrastructure of urban in life in New York City during the late 1970s, hip-hop culture—the music, aesthetic, dance, and visual art known as tagging and graffiti—provided a mode of communication and exchange for typically disenfranchised young people. Hip-hop is not the first cultural form to wrestle with the existential and ontological difficulties and limits marking the (post)modern period. Yet, it does so with a type of rawness and through imaginaries that push thought about and experience of the world beyond affected representations. The traumas and angst of the world are expressed in graphic form. In certain ways, hip-hop culture offers a new language, an alternate grammar and vocabulary for articulating the nature and meaning of life. In other words, the various genres of rap—what might be described as status rap, socially conscious rap, and gangsta rap—offer perspectives on this basic arrangement: how does one make life meaningful within the context of a world that does not respond to our wants and desires but instead is a place we experience as the absurd? Within rap music there are strong representations of this absurdity, with perhaps the most compelling being death. Humanists are well aware of death; we know the science behind it, and are quite reasonable and logical with respect to it. We will return to death in another chapter, but for now it suffices to say we live in cultural worlds that are not fully explained by means of scientific formulas. Our living toward death requires a particular cartography, a peculiar map that marks out the cultural contours of our existence. And for this, we should turn to hip-hop in that there are ways in which it promotes significant attention to the tensions and paradox associated with efforts to map out life structures within a context marked by the look, feel, and smell of death. It offers a compelling way of describing and addressing the grotesque dimensions of our demise that are much too graphic for most polite, humanist conversations.

Through a creative signifying of dominant strategies for life and more graphic modes of expressing life meaning within the context of absurdity, hip-hop marks a demand for visibility in a world more comfortable with invisibility. It has offered a way of speaking about and speaking to the tragic nature of human existence, without surrender to the nihilism theistic figures often fear. Instead, it provides comfort with paradox and an imagining of marginality as place for transformation.

Whereas hip-hop has turned status as a despised and troubling but short-term fad into a powerful tool for shaping cultural worlds across a global geography (e.g., think of Jay Z, "P Diddy," and Kanye West), humanist movements have not been as fortunate in their effort to create status and more transnational influence.

A hip-hop posture for humanists

Humanists are trying to fix this situation through public conversation and praxis, and through organizational infrastructure expanding beyond North America. However, there is a flaw in this approach in that such effort tends to involve strategies tied (at least loosely) to the methods and logic associated with the civil rights movement of the mid-twentieth century. These methods and this logic require acceptance of an assumption that moral outrage made visible constitutes the means for advancement. There is in this arrangement belief that progress is somehow linear and human history purpose driven. I am not pushing for rejection of the civil rights movement and, of course, humanists are not alone in appealing for inspiration to this process and this particular moment of struggle. After all, some important shifts in policy resulted from that movement. Yet, there are ways in which appeal to mid-twentieth-century techniques may not be the best strategy for the godless. For instance, popular imagination around the civil rights movement is overwhelmingly (but not of necessity) connected to a romanticizing of certain communities of struggle—for example, churches.

The rhetoric used to articulate that civil right struggle draws from the language of those particular communities. In addition, left in place after the civil rights movement is an ethical posture toward the world based on a privileging of supernatural claims/assumptions, a spiritual ontology, as well as an accompanying sense of sanctity afforded theism that humanists fight. Why maintain an approach to transformation of thought and quality of life that historically has privileged some of the very things humanists hope to eliminate?

Instead, humanists might take seriously as a source of information and strategy the best of hip-hop's framing of and posture toward sociocultural and political struggle. And, this process might begin with several considerations related to a posture toward the nature and meaning of the humanist movement as well as its self-understanding and its work. I would like to offer three examples of this rethinking.

Example one: "Thick" diversity

Hip-hop culture has demonstrated an impressive ability to trouble rigid cultural boundaries of nation/states and in this way promote diversity of expression, opinion, and so on. To speak of hip-hop is to mention an array of racial and ethnic groups—each with celebrated contributions to its development. There is a depth and thickness to diversity as modeled by hip-hop culture—despite some of its shortcomings. And while humanists voice an interest in diversity—and in certain ways promote it—such effort tends to produce what I will call *performative diversity*.

By this phrase I mean symbolic appreciation for "difference" as a marker of strength. It produces more *visible* "minority" communities of humanists, but this does little to change decision-making and the array of concerns promoted within these movements, and how these concerns are arranged and ranked. Yet, as hip-hop culture has demonstrated, more substantive diversity requires producing an organic system of symbols and signs that draws from the sensibilities of a wide-ranging group of participants. Adherents, so to speak, have to see themselves reflected in the workings of movements, see themselves as having real potential for involvement (e.g., leadership positions that shape the form and content of movements), and having the humanist movement lexicon reflect their language of life. Getting to this point requires changes to internal workings and also recruitment strategies.

In some cases, direct confrontation has increased numbers; however, the assumption that such tactics work in every context is a type of arrogance and disregard for cultural nuance. Not many African Americans, however, leave churches because of direct confrontation. To think so shows ignorance concerning the late twentieth-century patterns of growth for black churches—patterns that have little to do with theological commitment and more to do with networking opportunities and cultural connections. Simply denouncing and ridiculing Christian theology and belief does little to persuade: What do humanists offer as alternate sources of networking and cultural community?

As I have said elsewhere in this volume, the assumption reason can trump theology fails to recognize the manner in which theology mutates and theism (e.g., Christian churches) transforms itself. Its contemporary manifestations are less rigid than the pre-Enlightenment theologizing targeted in humanist critiques. Talk of the end of religion also fails to acknowledge regional differences and ignores new (and successful) religious formulations such as the Prosperity Gospel and the mega-churches adhering to it. These churches do not fall victim to typical critiques in that the most glaring examples of bad thinking are softened, and instead they highlight the Bible as a tool for advancing one's economic goals.

Again, theism is flexible, and does not die easy. While attempting to dismantle it, humanists must also recognize the short-term need to work in ways to lessen the negative impact it has on quality of life.

If readers think I am wrong, think again. The "look" of the typical humanistic gathering and the perpetual asking of the "how do we recruit people of color" questions do more than suggest I am right. Deconstruction of theism's flaws is required, but that must be followed by constructive projects and conversations that actually offer alternatives.

Smash the idols, but replace them with deeply human and compelling meaning-making opportunities and platforms.

Humanist approaches have suffered from an underlying assumption that there is one way to promote humanism, but this is wrong because people are messy, and communities are difficult to capture. And so, the godless should think in terms of multiple approaches to their work—an array of strategies that mirror the complexities of human social arrangements. Thinking this way and acting in light of such a philosophy of engagement might also cut down on the amount of infighting experienced within the humanist movement. But again, this requires an organic language—a vocabulary and grammar robust and descriptive enough to capture the imagination of humanists across various lines of tactical difference and constructive enough to translate to those outside their groups.

Example two: Significance of the ordinary[4]

It is often the case that humanists, in order to expand their presence and counter the foolishness of theistic orientations, highlight the unusual, the atypical and grand figures and moments within the history of their movement. Or, when the ordinary is highlighted it is juxtaposed to what is considered the markers of greatness. I would suggest such a move does not serve them well. Humanists, instead, should give more attention to the significance, the invaluable importance, of the mundane and the ordinary. I am not suggesting humanists fail to ritualize major life developments and challenges (Think in terms of the eighth essay in the volume.); rather, I am arguing even these rituals must remain committed to the importance of the mundane, and in this way provide means by which to appreciate (as individuals and in communities) the wonders of everyday life. This is one of the strong contributions humanists make to social existence—an unwillingness to look beyond the stuff of mundane existence, an unwillingness to demand the extraordinary as the only valuable marker of importance.

This has been one of the lasting contributions of hip-hop to the construction of cultural worlds. It is preoccupied with the ordinary, with the everyday and mundane patterns and moments of life, and it seeks to provide a lexicon for discussing and moving through those moments. In this way, it tackles head on the moments of discomfort, of paradox, of uncertainty that trouble—and by so doing it provides means by which to address the complexities of life. What such a move might allow is an earthy basis for our ethics. And, hip-hop teaches valuable lessons—both positive and negative—concerning the people involved in these efforts and the sociocultural arrangements through means of which these people move through the world.

Bodies are real in that they live and die, and humanistic ethics should be concerned with the consequences and connotations of this realness. The humanism message, borrowing some cues from hip-hop, might be the beauty of its ordinariness, the value of simple moments and events—and the need to appreciate this dimension of our existence—as individuals and in relationship. Doing so will trouble some humanists in that it means forgetting about some of the images of their godless liberalism. For example, on too many occasions, nontheists will proclaim that they do not see race; they do not give attention to difference in that way. They wear this proclamation like a blue ribbon—not realizing it is a statement representing a problem, not a solution. Antiblack racism and other modes of embodied discrimination are not challenged and fought by ignoring them, as if difference must be caste as a problem. Rather, hip-hop's approach to difference is much healthier, much more realistic in that hip-hop culture understands difference not as a dilemma to solve but as a benefit that serves to enhance creativity, expand knowledge and perspective, and shape cultural connections in healthier and productive ways. So, see race. One gains nothing by pretending not to see "colors." This illusion expends a lot of mental energy, generates a lot of social anxiety, and does not impress "racial minorities" (. . . minorities only if we fail to think globally).

Example three: Measured realism

In place of outcome-driven systems, a humanist ethical outlook might locate success in the process.[5] That is to say, continue to work. Humanists maintain this effort because they have the potential to effect/affect change, and they measure the value of their work not in terms of outcomes achieved but in the process of struggle itself. Regarding this, I am in agreement with ethicist and senior fellow with the Institute for Humanist Studies, Sharon Welch. There is no foundation for moral action that guarantees individuals and groups will act in "productive" and liberating ways, nor that they will ultimately achieve their objectives. Therefore, ethical activity is risky or dangerous because it requires operating without the certainty and security of a clearly articulated "product."[6] This is a more sober—some might argue a less passionate approach to ethics. It understands that human relationships (with self, others, and the world) are messy, inconsistent, and thick with desires, contradictions, motives, and a hopeful hopelessness.[7]

Humanistic ethical engagement should mirror the complexity and layered nature of the issues at hands. But as it currently stands humanists, and traditional theists, share an unfortunate and unsupported posture of optimism. The reason for the optimism differs for these two camps: God for them and science/reason for humanists. I am not pointing to the equating of God with forms of scientism (although this type of poor depiction of science does exist). Rather, I am suggesting that both traditional theists and humanists assume beneficial efforts to their actions—for them this is based on the balancing work done by the divinity; and for humanists it is premised on the assumption of science and reasonable thought as slow but steady resolutions to our problems. Isn't it in part because of this assumption so many humanists proclaim the demise of religion and the reign of reason? Both positions are too optimistic, but hip-hop culture offers a more balanced perspective—something I have on many occasions referenced as measured realism.

Hip-hop culture provides important lessons on the need for measured realism—a sense that human progress involves a paradox: advancement within a larger context of pain and misery. There must be awareness that human progress is not victim free, and it is not inevitable. That is to say, leave certainty to the theists; let their mythological protectors espouse overly optimistic pronouncements of future glory. Humanists should be in a better position than they to see the world as it is and to undertake a much more mature posture toward our work in the world. Humanists have not yet met the challenge, but they should: what is the look of ethical conduct when their efforts are just as likely to fail as to succeed?

Hip-hop culture provides a way of thinking about this question, of moving through life without guaranteed outcomes. Like hip-hop culture, humanists might learn to embrace the tragic quality of life and take from it a sobering regard for both their potential and their shortcomings. From this approach they might just come to a better and deeper appreciation of humanity.

Finally . . .

Some readers will disagree with my assessment, and some will resist giving hip-hop culture such a prominent role in their thinking. Even this disagreement if seriously engaged and interrogated might just point humanists in the direction of new and creative approaches to humanist thought and efforts. My goal is merely to suggest the importance of a particular conversation, to point out the weak spots in humanist mechanisms for understanding and acting out humanism. And, hip-hop culture points the way.

10

End of the "End": Humanism, hip-hop, and death

The importance of hip-hop as a hermeneutic and as a conceptual framework for reenvision humanism as well as its response to pressing concerns continues in this chapter. However, rather than considering the larger complex of hip-hop *culture*, I here limit myself to rap music as a type of heuristic device. And I combine this attention to rap music with the moralist thought of Albert Camus in order to explore the nature and meaning of death from a humanist perspective.

My purpose in doing this is to expose long-standing effort to render death abnormal to the extent it is perceived to push against what is right and acceptable about human be*ing*. In place of this thinking, I suggest death should lose its distinctiveness and become less easily distinguished from what we call life. In this regard, one might think in terms of material, "physical life/death" as opposed to a much clearer distinction such as "life . . . and then death." I conceptually ground this by means of a simple idea: To some extent, anthropology must entail a type of thanatology.[1] That is to say, to study humans and human society is to also study death.

Death is a constant that impinges upon all modalities of existence and through which we believe we ultimately bow to the limits of knowledge and be*ing*. So, it speaks a popular idea: human life is within limits and those restrictions can be acknowledged and through technological advances pushed, but they cannot be denied nor exceeded.

A few words on context

I spent a good number of years in Christian ministry, with one of my professional obligations being the ritualization of death—that is, giving eulogies, burials, comforting the living, and so on—all meant to address the fundamental point above regarding death.

Beyond the scope of the pulpit and the discourse extending from that source of authority, expressive culture in general points to bodies as subject to death. For example, within African American culture, from the early spirituals and folk narratives during the period of slavery forward, African Americans have used modalities of cultural expression to do a different type of work—an aesthetically contrived rebellion. Along these lines, W. E. B. Du Bois argued that artistic production had to serve a larger purpose, had to speak to the human struggle for advancement (in their case racial justice). Yet, Du Bois—and he is not alone in this—addressed personal confrontation with demise through artistic production that did not necessarily produce racial equality (i.e., public protest), but it did speak to the nature of death. For instance, his literary reflection on the death of his son in *The Souls of Black Folk* says something about an epistemology of meaning that confronts death not as something dehumanizing, but rather as a marker of our human connection—the integrity and weight of human relationship.[2]

Beyond what Du Bois offers, attention to death, of course, includes the example of brutal and reasonless destruction justified simply by the fact that African Americans *are* and are available as objects manipulated so as to support the social-political status quo. One need only to think in terms of death chronicled in the Travyon Martin murder discussed in another chapter, or the haunting song "Strange Fruit" by Billie Holiday that comes years before Martin.[3] That young man and that song along with less graphic examples map how African American expressive culture describes black bodies as always exposed to death. The fragility of the embodied body as a biochemical reality that is born, lives, and dies is not denied within those cultural examples. Even deals with cosmic forces—as is alleged to have taken place with blues artist Robert Johnson—do not deny death but rather give life within its parameters a particular robustness or charge.[4] Death still comes and conversation about this coming is not "sequestered."[5] In this regard, death—however it manifests—pushes into the public workings of the nation and pesters the private arrangements of life.

Death over against life

The locations for death and the framing of death have altered in light of a variety of socioeconomic, political, and cultural shifts in collective life over the centuries. Yet, something related to the awareness of death remains in place and undergirds reflective awareness of life's vulnerability. We live with the understanding and presence of an assumed end to physical existence.[6] There have been efforts, of course, to control, monitor, and ritualize material death (the end of vital biological functions)—in some ways to privatize it so as to make it manageable, to make it easy as understood within a particular sociocultural understanding, and to render it over against life.

Death experienced in this form gives the person time, resource, and opportunity to work out "arrangements" in a way consistent with individual need/want and in light of communal assumptions and priorities. It might involve arrangement of resources, nurturing relationships, and so on. This is an economy of death that is manageable and to some extent "owned" by humans. The opposite of this, the type of death avoided, involves a hard death that is untimely (outside the socially assumed chronological frame for human life), death that is violent or in some other way outside the pattern of life/death desired by the person, or death that for any other reason is outside the dominate narrative of "life . . . and then death."

This framing offers death as disruptive of sociocultural arrangements that mark out life or physical being within a given community. In this way, physical death produces *dis*-ease within a community and fosters a certain type of anxiety within individuals. Even in theistic traditions, such as Christianity that often pose death as transition to new life, death remains a problem of sorts in that it is a sign of human flaw—the conclusion to human shortcomings. Would humans experience death, as we know it if not for humanity straying away from God and being forced out the Garden of Eden:

> Cursed is the ground because of you; through painful toil you will eat food from it all the days of your life. It will produce thorns and thistles for you,
> and you will eat the plants of the field. By the sweat of your brow you will eat your food until you return to the ground, since from it you were taken; for dust you are and to dust you will return.[7]

While we may experience a form of "transcendence" (a difficult word for me to use here) as we live in the memories of those left behind, physical confrontation with the world (i.e., "life") comes to an end. If this statement just made were expressed as a written text, it might appear something like this: l/i/f/e. And so, there is a beginning and an end—with slippage between clearly identified markers of time and space—after which the meaning of that particular person is only a memory, which is an unreliable series of ideas arranged with intent and historical purpose. "In the last analysis," as has been written, "human societies are merely men and women banded together in the face of death."[8]

Yet, there is another way to think about this issue of death. Instead of understanding death as a problem of being—that is, existing in opposition to life—some rap artists suggest it is a matter of proportion—that is, death as connected to life.

Rap music on death: Tupac is Jesus

Like the blues, rap music makes use of the traditional language and grammar associated with mourning of loss, and of other modalities of emotional and psychic pain linked with physical death. However, in addition, rap music has altered the tools of discourse by giving terms new epistemological arrangements and concerns. In some instances this involves not simply a signifying of sociocultural categories of relationality, but also manipulation of religious figures with the aim of having them do a different work. For instance, there is Tupac Shakur's "Black Jesus," a paradigmatic figure discussed elsewhere in this volume.

As Albert Camus reminds us, talk of mechanisms of transformation, stories of transcendence and change all lead to the same end, to the same conclusion—the overlap between life and death and the presence of absurdity either fought or embraced. This is a different knowledge of death. It is not marked by wallowing in fear of death, but instead involves recognition of death as already wrapped in life. A similar recounting, I think, is present in Tupac Shakur's "Blasphemy" and "Hail Mary," two tracks from the same CD that speak to a new understanding of death. Similar to the converted missionary in Camus's story "The Renegade, or a Confused Mind"—converted from Christianity to worship of a fetish—these tracks turn religion inside out. Its value and meaning, its expression, and goals are altered so as to reject its certainties of a future lodged in hope in favor of familiarity with the absurdity of death/life. Pain and redemption are merged and rendered indistinguishable. And, listeners (and readers for Camus) are confronted with a choice to make: when and how is death? Material death is juxtaposed to a new epistemology of death.[9]

With Tupac, death is absorbed—not dismissed or feared—taken in as a part of life. In his words, "This Thug Life will be the death of me."[10] He, as a Christ figure, offers a system of analysis and of engagement that does not betray the content of death. Rather than fear or avoidance as the grammar of death as presented in the dominant and guiding logic of death as problem of being, Tupac embraces death as knowledge of life. In at least two cases he accomplishes this by retelling Christian stories of "life . . . and then death." In this retelling God is displaced by another—a new prophet who is in line with the logic of the thug and for whom death is not a condition to be fixed. This process of counter-theology begins with a recasting of the Christ Event:

> Tell me I ain't God's son, nigga mom a virgin;
> We got addicted had to leave the burbs, back in the ghetto;
> Doin' wild shit . . .[11]

And, this new Christ, this "Black Jesus," has his own miracles to perform. Moses, Tupac reminds, may have split a sea but he, Black Jesus, "split the blunt and rolled the fat one. I'm deadly, Babylon beware."[12]

Linked in the song above are revenge and desire, the assertion of self as acknowledgment of something valuable within the person—something worthy of protection and safeguarding.[13] This establishes epistemological grounding for the parallels he sets between himself and Jesus the Christ. The latter is pulled from his privileged station and Tupac—the "Black Jesus"—takes his place alongside God. As Tupac says, "All eyes on me."[14] What is more, Tupac notes that "Only God Can Judge Me," but what does that mean for the God/man? It must be remembered that he exists with God, as the new Christ. Hence, he judges himself because he has dismantled through word and deed the logic undergirding perceptions of life and death through the structuring of meaning *qua* THUG LIFE—a type of glorious, chaotic, march through the world—defiance. It is a symbolic gripping of his balls as Jay Z (the one accused of demonic deals and conspiracies articulated through signs and symbols) might describe the accompanying posture.[15] Tupac's throne is equal to God's but it touches both heaven and earth.

While I do not read Tupac as a Christian, he is not necessarily a humanist or atheist. That is, he reframes (but keeps) the location and function of God.[16] For example, in certain circles conversation concerning the life of Tupac Shakur after he is shot and presumed dead continues.[17] In a word, some continue to believe he is not dead, but is away, preparing for his return. Tupac is the embodiment of life/death.

Both Tupac and Camus recognize such a repositioning as a matter of blasphemy—a certain defiant posture toward rebellion. Adopting this posture, Tupac cautions listeners not to push him or provoke him because "revenge is like the greatest joy next to gettin' pussy."[18] In a certain sense, Tupac *qua* "Black Jesus" reincarnates the rebel who brings into question assumptions concerning the basis of knowledge related to death and the accompanying focus of ethics. Put another way, and drawing loosely from Camus's construction, "Black Jesus" recognizes rebellion as needed by all.[19] In a word, it is rebellion on behalf of and for a much larger audience by means of which death is conquered through removal of any assumption that it constitutes a crisis of being—life's end. Death, "where is your sting?"[20]

The answer is written on and through Tupac's body: death, then, is already and always.

Tupac normalizes death in that he claims a connection to God, for example, the ultimate structuring of meaning. That is to say, Tupac makes death a matter of life by taking from it any abstraction. Even his body—marked with tattoos speaking to this new reality—presents an alternate epistemology of meaning. It is a new message, but like those tattoos across his body, it has a certain type of permanency.[21] The ink may fade, but the new message will always call attention to itself, and seeing his body will force a particular epistemological dissonance. He offers his flesh as a new communion into life to death and death to life. The tattoos mark the way.[22]

The success of Tupac's effort is not of concern to me because it is not the measure of importance from my perspective. That is to say, theology is altered through his narrative (as well as others like it) in that historical lucidity trumps "mysticism"—hard living in the "hood" over Gnosticism and Esotericism. There are recognized values—for example, Tupac's THUG LIFE—but these constitute a particular framing of meaning and ethics that cuts against the structures of reality meant to foster death as a problem of being. Christianity is dismantled and replaced by a new measure of reality.

The first Christ turns the other check, accepts offense for the sake of something greater, and does so with an eye toward death as a transitional affair. The Black Jesus, however, responds to offense and recognizes the importance of attention to an alternate gospel that privileges those very things the dominant society pretends to reject regarding life/death. An epistemology supporting death as the end of reality is replaced by an alternate knowing that gives priority to the weight of human existence as a matter of living into death.[23] What ideology or even theology can be employed to hold together this type of ontological contradiction? Even the question serves to shatter the illusion, to break through efforts to control what really cannot be controlled, to banish death and restrict its presence to a select "location" segregated and despised.

Rap music and death: New authority

Tupac challenges the arrangements of death by claiming divinity—claiming control over the construction of life/death. This is something of an ontological move, whereas artists Jay Z and Kanye West in "No Church in the Wild" question the nature of authority with implication for epistemologies of life and death.[24] The brilliance of this piece—besides the intrigue generated in light of the strong opposition to it from certain, predictable quarters—is its fundamental challenge to the basis of Western knowledge, morality, and ethics. By dismantling the sources of this authority represented by the people gathered as a mob, the king, and God, all falls to the will of the unbeliever—the one who refuses to sanction the prime Unity, as Camus might name it, used to hold in place modalities of subjugation. The track's chorus frames this thinking as a question:

> What's a mob to a king? What's a king to a God?
> What's a God to a nonbeliever who don't believe in anything?[25]

Meaning is premised on consent and agreement without the assurance of an overarching guide: "We formed a new religion," raps West, "no sins as long as there's permission."[26] One might even suggest this unbeliever is Camus's rebel, one with lucidity and awareness; or in the words of Jay Z and West "watch the throne."[27] Like Camus's rebel, this unnamed destroyer of illusion in "No Church in the Wild," faces the absurd, does not surrender to it, but instead moves through the world valuing struggle and guided by awareness of the illusions meant to hold humans in place. And like the rebel, there is no effort to forge a revolution—a new structuring of meaning that wipes out anew dignity, integrity, and death. As Montaigne encourages, this rebel, the protagonist in "No Church in the Wild" likely will be found working when death comes. Both, again as Montaigne encourages, are learning to die. Death, all three—Kanye West, Jay Z, and Montaigne—seem to know, should not be feared but recognized as life.[28]

If death as problem of being requires acceptance of authority, a surrender to the logic of dominance, Jay Z and Kanye West push against this structuring of reality and find meaning in meaninglessness, thereby dismantling the prevailing Unity of ideas undergirding death as anything other than life/death. Those embracing this sense of death become the marker of the real, the measure of prosperity, control over aesthetics, acquisition of "goods," physical prowess, and so on—important markers of meaning within the United States. In other words, they expose the "real." Other formulations are without authority and are signified by rendering death the marker of life in an absurd world, or the "jungle."

Can death as a problem of being withstand this challenge to its logic, form, and function?

A prime marker of this system of reality, the housing for its prime form of authority, the church, has no place within the world constructed by Jay Z and Kanye West, where authority is not surrendered to another but is established in connection to others. That is to say, they urge listeners to live into death—just "ball" until it is over. In crude terms, according to Jay Z, "ball so hard, this shit crazy; Y'all don't know that don't shit phase me."[29]

This is the new epistemology of life/death—the retaking of authority, the establishment of new ground rules. Embedded in this is a call to recognize "greatness" along new lines that blast truncated notions of death.[30]

This move on their part is enough to disrupt the nature of death to the extent it troubles the epistemology justifying and the ontology shaping death as a problem of be*ing*.

By means of this turn, forms of authority that sanction and buttress poor thinking on death are disrupted and the sacred nature of this logic that distances humans from death is challenged. Authority is toppled, and it is not replaced with anything that can offer the same type of unity of meaning.[31] "No Church in the Wild" raises questions, strong questions, and uses them to topple the structuring of life and meaning. The final process of authority rest with "nonbelievers" whose stance (e.g., rejection or perhaps rebellion) calls into question all that is dependent on consent to death as separation. Sacred markers and mechanisms of authority are dismantled, and the secular reigns! And, what falls as a result of this shift is the framing of a wrongful death.

Looking at death

Harlem Renaissance writer Richard Wright, in "The Man Who Lived Underground," speaks to a similar arrangement of meaning (but without the same intent). The protagonist, Fred Daniels, who is in the sewer hiding from the police accused of a crime he did not commit, uses darkness to enter from below ground into a movie theater. He is as dismissive of these delusion seekers as he is of the delusional Church folks he encountered from below their sanctuary.[32] Yet, he is more like them than he can initially admit. He thinks his presence underground has altered him, made him ghost-like and untouchable as he moves from surface to sewer. But there are too many instances when this line of reasoning is broken, when his presence is real, substantive, but not quite human. His is not a death that constitutes a problem of being—a clear distinction from living. Daniels' final encounter with police officers when he tries to explain his circumstances—as if he is human to them—points to this fact and their action—to shot him—is meant to confine death as physical control, social regulation (i.e., law and order), and ontological positioning. Readers learn, as Daniels experiences this violence, death bleeds into life and life into death.

What Wright offers is thought provoking on a variety of levels, yet it is with greater appeal that the cultural worlds produced by certain rap artists subvert bad notions of death by giving explicit attention to death, and by promoting the end of the "end" in ways that trouble or challenge typical religious markers of an "after" death. The girt and misery surrounding death is not given a theological gloss as one finds in the spirituals or slave narratives, sermons, and prayers, for instance, but rather is left raw and harsh. One of the early anthems of hip-hop—"The Message" by Grand Master Flash and the Furious Five—speaks to the perpetual presence of the smells, sights, sounds, and feel of decay, of decline within the arenas of life.

> It's like a jungle sometimes
> It makes me wonder how I keep from goin' under.[33]

And I say, amen to this perception of life/death.

Rap artists like those named above offer a graphic and poetic response that crushes theodical responses to death; in fact, they hint at the transformation of anthropology into thanatology. Humanists can learn a great deal from them: maintain the tension, recognize the absurd, and work through an effort to accept the importance of life within a context of death.

11

Speaking in public: The problem of theistic language for collective life

Having given attention to various dimensions of humanism with/in cultural worlds, I now turn attention to the issue of language—the grammar and vocabulary used to express public life. I do so by turning to the presidency of Barack Obama and the challenges associated with it regarding the relationship of race and religion to the cultural expression of life in public. In this way, this final chapter serves to tie together the various components of this volume—race (on the level of the group and the individual), religion (what it is and how it impacts public life), and culture (signs and symbols used to articulate a vision of life)—and pulls them into public view.

The President

The presidency of Barack Obama has received a great deal of attention. One of the more charged elements of this attention involved Rev. Jeremiah Wright and liberation theology. Reporters and journalists asked questions during President Obama's first run for the White House: Does the anger in Rev. Wright's response to racism and his use of the work of liberation theologians such as James Cone (who are deeply critical of white supremacy and who say God is "black") point to a position that is "anti-American"? And, how influenced by this thinking was Barack Obama?

President Obama's rise to the highest position of authority in the United States has generated debate concerning the connections between race, religion, and politics. Many have debated in writing the nature and meaning of these connections, including ethicist Gary Dorrien, who entered the conversation with his book titled *The Obama Question*.[1] Emerging out of liberal theism's legacy, that text explores how those committed to Christian faith in a progressive manner might understand President Obama and his decision-making.

The book hits its highpoint as Dorrien begins to frame Obama's presidency explicitly in line with markers of religious progressivism—a commitment to the disadvantaged and a clear message of social justice. At that point, near the end of the book, the tone and texture of religious left's sensibilities are most vibrant, and the tensions in President Obama's thinking are most apparent. As Dorrien notes, the Reverend Jeremiah Wright controversy surfaced the form(s) of Christian engagement marking Obama's perception of human accountability and human potential to act in life-affirming ways, in light of the promise and pitfalls of twenty-first-century political maneuverings.

President Obama's embodiment of a complex, layered, and fluid identity and his rhetoric of hard-fought possibility have exposed the shortcomings of US democratic processes. That is to say, President Obama's personal history could be read in a variety of ways: Based on his parents—is he African American or not? Based on his name—is he Christian or Muslim? Based on having lived in a variety of locations and countries—is he truly American and committed to "our" way of life? Furthermore, responses to his actions on both the "right" and "left" show the US political system tainted by unresolved difficulties with difference (e.g., race and so on). The manner in which it is marred by shortsighted discussions of the "good" and the nature of morality capable of pushing the US nation toward its "better self" is glaring.

Speaking the USA

While neither seems willing to acknowledge this, both the religious right and the religious left have fallen short with respect to these ideological challenges. For instance, both social ethicist and political activist of the twentieth-century Reinhold Niebuhr and the late minister and advocate of conservative, Bible-based morality Jerry Falwell showed little creativity and little insight regarding the politics of difference and the difference of politics.[2] For instance, both Niebuhr and Falwell failed to recognize the impact of race and racism on life in the United States in ways that were unspoken and embedded in the political and cultural fabric of the United States. Both camps—the "right" and the "left"—have done little to enhance the workings of the public arena of discourse to the extent they have failed to wrestle with the full range of sociopolitical and cultural challenges that face the United States. Instead, they, in their own ways, fed into a sense of the United States as a special, exceptional nation with a destiny of greatness to be secured at the expense of others, if necessary.

This is not to suggest religious progressives march into their public activities to the same drumbeat as the religious-political right. They are different, as Niebuhr and Falwell were different in their thinking and commitments. Yet, the religious right and the religious left draw from the same source materials—scripture and so on—although they interpret them differently. Both camps are optimistic; yet, if Dorrien is correct, little about the politics of collective life has changed as a consequence of this optimism and the actions it has encouraged. In other words, there is embedded in theistically inspired thinking an optimism of a greater weight than bodies can carry—a grand language of transformation that dwarfs the human ability to "do." Humans want to achieve more than our capacities actually will allow.

Theistically inspired optimism wants to deny the nature of politics as simply arrangements of human potential and limitation, a system of bargaining that gives a charge to the dynamics of human relationships that both highlights and downplays difference. This optimism pushes those holding it to find in political maneuverings the outline of some deeper concern for life—a destiny that speaks to our internal greatness wanting to flow outward. And so, the religious left and the right are both frustrated.

In both cases, there is something wrong with religious optimism and the way in which it prevents necessary recognition of the tragic nature of life—the shortcomings and disappointments that arise despite our best efforts. The religious language of biblically based optimism espoused by figures such as Reinhold Niebuhr, Martin Luther King, Jr, and so on fails to recognize this reality. We need something beyond this particular religious vocabulary and grammar.

There are ways in which the presidency of Barack Obama calls for a new way of talking about collective hopes and concerns—a language yet to be created. Through such a new way of talking about public life we recognize both possibilities and limitations. And, we recognize we cannot simply think about these limitations as some type of stain or limitation of our soul. The problem may be the failure of our public moral values and visions, but this is mundane and not the consequence of sickness of the soul.

In more concrete terms, the tension between advancement and stagnation raises a question not only concerning political will, but it also begs the question of the religious left's ability to forge an adequate grammar for political change. If anything, the typical and shopworn vocabulary for collective effort and public life shows through the inability to capture President Obama with the usual language of progressivism or conservatism. Perhaps the tensions within the Obama presidency stem not from political naïveté but rather point to the limits of religious optimism, and the boundaries of (Christian) religiously inspired language of progress? Perhaps this religious optimism and the public conversation and action it generates are not enough to advance public life in healthy and nurturing ways. It is all to possible—and I would argue probable— that advancement of democratic ideals in public life requires something beyond the certainties offered in biblical stories and liberal theologies.

As the debate surrounding President Obama suggests, this new language— this way of talking about life within the public arena—is not in place, but working to develop it is a worthy endeavor. I simply want to note the importance, the necessity, of working to construct new ways of describing and discussing public life in the United States that appreciate the complexities of its history and that recognize both national limitations and possibilities.

President Obama's first inauguration address briefly mapped out a geography of belonging that included a fuller range of religious and philosophical perspectives running from nontheists to theists. To the extent it forced a momentary reckoning with the competing life orientation claims lodged in the United States, this "opening up" has been of some value. Yet, it did little to address the vocabulary and grammar used to shape and present the sense of "life, liberty, and happiness" operative in so many quarters. How does one present "life, liberty, and happiness" within the context of competing faith claims with differing perspectives on, for example, the nature of the humans who are undertaking such pursuits and claiming these rights? For instance, much of the undergirding thought for these pursuits and claims rest on a soft theism; yet, what is the "look" of this pursuit (and the nature of happiness) when not buttressed by theism but instead by the "nonbelief," as President Obama put it, of some citizens?

The limits of language

I make an effort to address such questions through a centering of embodied life, the meaning of occupation of time and space, as the framework of discussions concerning the nature of existence defined by "life, liberty, and the pursuit of happiness." As a nation, the United States has mapped out the geography for and content of life with respect to the activities and conversations that promote pleasure; and it has made this configuration a basic right associated with citizenship. What remains a persistent issue is public discussion concerning the markers of the pleasurable: what is the proper language for describing it?

Developments in the public, political debate in the United States over the past several years point not only to the continuing dilemma of race (class and other markers of difference used to harm) in this country, but also suggest the inadequate connection between the traditional grammar of political obligation and opportunity, and the "look" of our political wants and needs. That is to say, for instance, the Tea Party and other modalities of political and "moral" recalibration seek to use a strict and restricting grammar of Christian obligation as a way of framing the content and intent of, say, the US Constitution. Claiming to represent the spirit and purpose of liberty and freedom that have defined this country and were symbolized by the Boston Tea Party, contemporary "tea partiers" promote a conservative view of US internal and external dealings. While maintaining the pretense of openness to all committed to the welfare of this nation, regardless of race, religion, and so on, their framing of the Tea Party's meaning and work and their framing of the United States as a nation are premised on a language and grammar that uses the Christian faith as the basic conceptual paradigm. This is their language, their grammar, because they assert we *are* a Christian nation.

Although gaining some attention within political circles, the Tea Party Movement does not capture the full imagination of US citizens; yet, the appeal to Christian vocabulary and grammar as a way to articulate and translate basic principles of the US self-understanding pushes beyond this movement and is much older than it. Assuming this language of the Christian faith should mark (and has always marked) the intent and self-understanding of this nation, politicians and citizens from various political camps agree at least in soft (self-serving) ways that it should persist. Yet, it has not worked well; it has never worked well in that this language—the vision of collective life supported by this language—has not safeguarded the welfare of the collective community in all its diversity.

Christian language is too narrow, too "cosmic," and not grounded enough to serve as a way to organize the energy and needs of the United States, too narrow to give full and earthy meaning to "life, liberty, and the pursuit of happiness" that defines so much of self-understanding in this nation. The Christian faith, and its language by extension, is too grounded in a glance beyond this world; it seeks its meaning and approval beyond the confines of human history. In short, at its core, it is "other-worldly," and how can that type of language give full meaning to rather worldly—property inspired—concerns? US public life stands in need of a different way of speaking about the deepest desires of this nation, because those desires and wants are ultimately tied to physicality, to the material nature of existence, as opposed to being responsive to any type of spiritual or transcendent qualities.

Here is the problem: appeal to Christian language tends to assume basic desires as individuals within the context of a national community drawn from a relationship to transcendent concerns and meanings. However, the meaning of life, liberty, and happiness are actually biological, neurological—neurobiological—and not easily captured through traditional theological assumptions. Traditional

Christian theology—think what one hears in most churches—points in the wrong direction in that it takes focus off humans as simply biological creatures and seeks to frame them as something more significant, creators with a divine spark and purpose.

Even more worldly forms of theological thinking that begin to emerge during the late nineteenth and twentieth century with figures such as Rev. Walter Rauschenbusch and later Dr Martin L. King Jr are concerned with the world, but still view it as a somewhat imperfect resemblance to a more perfect cosmic reality that we must seek to secure. Their liberal theology—or social gospel—sought to model human interactions on the model of Jesus Christ, thereby giving Christians a way of addressing pressing issues of modern life by following the principles of Jesus' ministry. But even this points backward and understands the best of human want and human capacity as tied to a cosmic relationship. It fails to recognize the limited and deeply earthbound nature of human wants, desires, and pursuits. There is still in place the assumption that earthly activities are connected to unseen dramas and struggles—"powers and principalities"—impacting human life. This is not to say figures such as King did not appreciate human ethics and social structures; rather it is to say he still understood these things to be tied to transhistorical concerns and possibilities. His thinking, and that of others holding to similar positions, is premised on the assumption that there is something out there, something that is concerned with humans and in relationship to which people have described and arranged the workings and rules of our national life.

This way of thinking about basic aims as citizens of the United States has not served the citizenry well. It has ignored the real source of these desires for life, liberty, and happiness because it cast them as having some type of cosmic origin and function when, again, they are merely the result of our biology. We will not develop a useful and productive way of discussing the nature and function of these three desires if we do not first gain clarity concerning their relationship to which (or what) we are as biologically motivated creatures. Such a turn might give a better way of understanding the motivations for the central importance of and meaning behind guiding principles and ethics. And in better understanding them, citizens might be better equipped to safeguard their importance and opportunities to secure them.

Revising language

Recent studies that take complex neuroscience findings and make them available to a general public point out the complexities of our brain—the manner in which it actually holds within its mysteries the source of so much we once associated with spiritual essence and the like. This is to suggest, as *The Believing Brain* makes clear, these things are all a matter of belief; yet, these beliefs have no substantive metaphysical basis.[3] They are still a part of our biology and should be addressed as such. The real basis for our commonality, for our shared commitments, is not religiously grounded in any traditional sense—too many religious orientations in the United States for that—but instead is the result of shared biology: the brain shapes and monitors these desires and pursuits and it is this biological relatedness that ties all humans together. The working of the brain as geography for this structuring of the meaningful life is the shared basis for guiding principles and their hold on citizens. Hence, the language used to describe and explain these principles should be tied not to a particular religion but to the workings of shared humanity.

Theistic theology traditionally understood and arranged as a language for particular religious orientations is too limited and limiting for a proper sense of fundamental pursuits that ground quality of life. While transcendent forces might offer a convenient way of solidifying the authority of particular ideas, notions of god(s) do not adequately represent the shared "stuff" of human motivation for the safeguarding of the three principles noted so many times already in this brief chapter. The cosmic script offered through god(s) seldom changes in substantial ways, although human need and self-understanding do change. And while there may be something genetic about our religiosity as many philosophers and scientists now note, this does not mean a particular arrangement of this inclination beyond a general quest for profound life meaning should rule the day.

Life-framing principles are about meaning—the fostering of meaning through the framing of what most matters—but one should not attempt to describe or understand this in ways that downplay biology. That is, neurobiology, the fleshy nature of humanity is the source of human inclinations whether they are political, cultural, social, spiritual, and so on. One should be mindful of this when thinking about and seeking to formulate the mechanisms for accessing and securing the "stuff" of individual existence as the substance of rights as citizens. To say these things are God-given is not to point to something beyond ourselves, but to simply suggest that they are an outgrowth of our very biology—a dimension of our fundamental structure and this is what makes them compelling and long lasting on the group level.

Turning again to *The Believing Brain*, there is reason to believe the brain—or in general the physical workings of the human—is responsible for political inclinations and all their trappings, including the guiding politico-social arrangements of life such as the principles of life, liberty, and the pursuit of happiness. This being the case, no one religious grammar garnered from one of the dominant religious communions in the United States is adequate for speaking to or for the struggle regarding our deep yearning for these principles active within the context of both individual lives and communal existence. Hence, while religious orientation and belief structures may prove useful for the individual and the like-minded, they do not provide a language adequate as the mode of exchange within the public arena.

Linguistic building blocks

The challenge is to actually develop such a language, to gather such a grammar and vocabulary. Doing so requires at the very least tolerance, imagination, and a different perspective on difference. This is not to say religious commitment and theological vocabulary serve no purpose. They do, within certain confined dimensions of private (and communal) life. However, they are not expansive enough, do not capture enough of the landscape of life in the United States, to constitute the most viable way of naming and speaking about the goals of civic existence marked out within the context of an expansive national community. Such is the case because, as Benedict Anderson rightly notes, this national community is not based on direct contact but rather imagined connections, and these imagined connections are not defined by the workings of one particular theistic faith stance.[4] In fact, our understanding of shared human need and desire is not solved through greater clarity with respect to the workings of religion, but rather through a more profound understanding of how the brain works. The answer is in our materiality, in the relationship between biology and socio-anthropology. Religion is just one product of this brain at work and, arguably, not the most significant in that it often forces at least emotional distance from our bodies as biological.

Instead, a more humanistic approach to what is meant by life, liberty, and the pursuit of happiness is helpful in that it centers the human—as material and cultural reality. These three, in a general sense, have something to do with pleasure—how it is understood, shaped, and captured. And while various religious traditions might have a troubled relationship with pleasure, particularly the way in which it is dependent on the body which some traditions hold suspect as the site of all our troubles, pleasure and the desire for it are deeply human and components of individual and collective notions of fulfillment.

Navigation of the pathways of pleasure—the structuring and safeguarding of pleasure—is part of our wiring. It is fundamentally human and is more basic than the teachings or language of any particular religious tradition. These principles or "unalienable rights" are promoted in the Declaration of Independence as cornerstones of the pleasure of freedom. They belong to each person across an expansive geography of communities. How, then, can such far-reaching and fundamental rights be adequately defined and captured? Do they not require the conversation and exchange made possible by a more fundamental, a more humanistic, grammar—one that centers on the commonalities of our basic shared biology over against the irresolvable differences of theistic belief.

What I propose involves a clear dilemma—a need to recognize the possibility of tension between theistic readings of these three desires and nontheistic perceptions of the same. After all, both positions involve belief. Yet, I make a pitch for the nontheistic variety of belief in that theisms tend not to be institutionally and theologically flexible enough to shift quickly (or in real time) with expansion in knowledge. They are too rigid, not plastic enough. The response of so many religious communities to the demands for gay rights and protections under the law serves as just one example of what I mean. Pleasure, as *The Compass of Pleasure* makes clear, is tied to our brain chemistry and part of our neurophysiology.[5] Theism speaks to and about pleasure and makes an effort to forge a language for understanding and controlling it, but in rather truncated ways—ways that do not fully appreciate just how "earthbound" are both religion and pleasure. To have public discussions concerning pleasure outlined by "life, liberty, and the pursuit of happiness" requires a more expansive set of tools than offered by Christianity or any other theistic tradition. Needed are mechanisms of exchange more consciously stemming from an understanding of humanity as central and with less appeal to transcendence.

And here I repeat much of what I said in two *Religion Dispatches* articles from October 27, 2009 and February 13, 2009.[6] To the extent that it is possible (and many atheists will reject this suggestion), attention should be given to a search for common ethical ground that brackets the harsher presentations of both theistic and atheistic views. I am not asking for a "can't we all get along" rejection of debate and a suspension of aggressive wrestling over ideas. It is important to challenge beliefs as a way of safeguarding human accountability and integrity, but there must also be a push for more than destruction of all markers of religious commitment. Atheists and humanists should continue to interrogate and critique theistic orientations, and adherents of theistic positions should continue to challenge atheists. If not, careful and self-critical attention paid to science by some atheists and humanists, for instance, could easily become scientism—a faith of its own, with figures such as Richard Dawkins serving as its prophets.

History shows that reason may alter the posture of faith-based communities, may force them to shift their language and limit their size and their sociopolitical reach, but it will not destroy faith. The very definition of faith should make this apparent. Atheists and humanists miscalculate the core significance of theism if they assume it is about doctrine and creeds, ritual forms and physical structures; those things most often attacked. As I have noted elsewhere in this volume, theism, at its core, is about the making of meaning and the establishment of stories and practices related to how and why we occupy time and space; ritual, doctrines, sacred texts, and so on are only cultural manifestations of this deeper meaning. These rituals and doctrines are secondary, not primary: they are modified; they shift; they change to fit the historical-cultural context. Attacks on theism's theological or ritual shortcomings, while correct in some regards, will not end theism.

Theism and atheism/humanism will persist, and any real gains made toward healthy existence for our world must involve collaboration (not assimilation) and partnerships between moderates within both groups. This is not denial of difference and does not require rejection of one's chosen orientation. Rather it involves recognition that a mature approach to life rejects fundamentalism of any kind, and demands complex relationships of shared ethical commitment even when those relationships are burdened with tension. But the more difficult task involves development of the national posture necessary for achieving this vision. The problem is obvious; religious traditions involve competing faith claims, conflicting postures toward the practice of faith, and shifting assumptions concerning the public nature of religious commitment. Rich, "thick," and complex discourse requires new structures, new rules of engagement—a push beyond what marks the current and public framing of religious concerns and practices. Great care must be exercised, or what we will get is superficial "tolerance" of religious humanists and secularists, a sense of what it means to be religious in the United States that barely hides an assumed theistic, if not Christian, backstory.

Finally . . .

President Obama's call for recognition of religious diversity falls short, in that little thus far suggests a rethinking of how we in the United States define, arrange, and shape our fundamental concerns. There will be no questioning of our general assumptions concerning what is meant when the United States is referred to as a religious nation. There is an opportunity here that should not be missed. Rather than simply assuming a clear understanding of what it means to be "American" and "religious," here is a chance to interrogate the wide range of possibilities.

This involves sustained examination of what it means (and what must be surrendered) to embrace all modalities of religion within the context of this democracy. The signs of a morally and ethically centered and successful nation might need some rethinking in light of the various (and at times competing) norms held dear and celebrated within the context of religious diversity.

For the type of growth I suggest here, the nation will need a task force charged with helping politicians and civic leaders think about the nature and meaning of our nation's religious diversity. This group of scholars and leaders (both theistic and nontheistic) would be charged with developing a framework for addressing the intersections of public life by helping foster a language and posture for engagement in public conversation concerning the pleasures that matter to us most.

Epilogue: Sisyphus's happiness

This is not a book about Camus—not a humanistic interpretation of his writings. Yet, there is something for the godless, for humanists, in Camus's insights. Somewhere between absurdity and happiness is humanism. It is a life stance, a philosophy of life—or for some a religious orientation—that recognizes metaphysics but in such a way as to ground those questions of knowledge and being in the empirical. It urges ethics and moral codes that value the web of life, of which humanity is a small part, and assumes we work to improve the arrangements of collective (and individual) life without any sort of transcendent assistance.

Camus encourages us to project Sisyphus as not broken by this process of pushing a rock for eternity, but instead we should see him as content with the process of struggle, the ability to do something regardless of what that doing achieves. This is a strike against nihilism—a rejection of total meaninglessness, but rather a new type of hope—one applicable to humanists struggling to make sense of race, religion, and cultural production.

Even in the face of certain physical death (a living into death, actually), Camus advocates for ethics—for action derived from love and a desire to safe-guard dignity. Elsewhere in his work, he would even say, "Absurdity is King, but love saves us from it."[1] This is not love associated with a God or gods, with metaphysics that pulls us away from the empirical—from the feel, the taste, the touch, the sights, and smells of the world. No, this North African—Camus—is committed to movement through the world made possible only by the strength of human will and the integrity of our goals, although neither will be enough to win the day. Still, he notes, "one must imagine Sisyphus happy." Imagine, him—despite the absurd circumstances, the distain of the gods, a nonresponsive environment—*happy*.

In the very request to imagine him happy is the presence of the absurd: one, according to Camus, must imagine the "un/real"—and see what is not present. That is to say, Camus calls readers to push beyond what circumstances project and rebel. In a word, one is to see Sisyphus as living with/in the absurd nature of experience of the material world without being defined by that experience. He pushes the rock without "appeal,"[2] without a request for mercy, and with a robust sense of rebellion. The powers in charge may have thought this was a punishment—rolling the rock only to have it descend again—that would destroy any sense of control over circumstances and any measure of success or closure,[3] yet, Camus argues they were mistaken. In that moment when he has pushed it to the peak of the hill and right before it reverses and moves back done, there is a second of success. "At the very end of his long effort measure by skyless space and time without depth," Camus writes, "the purpose is achieved. Then Sisyphus watches the stone rush down in a few moments toward that lower world whence he will have to push it up again toward the summit. He goes back down to the plain."[4] Camus seems to concentrate on that moment as a celebration of rebellion or revolt, and he matches that moment with Sisyphus's tenacity in repeating the effort . . . as if Sisyphus really had a choice.

For the moralist, Camus, it is not the loss of freedom, the constraint on will that matters. Instead, it is the moment of lucidity, of awareness that makes Sisyphus "the absurd hero" and it is this awareness that renders his plight tragic. That clarity or awareness allows Sisyphus to own something of his situation and his response to it. Therefore, for Camus it is this awareness, the moment of consciousness that also marks our lives as absurd; and, like Sisyphus, this awareness in the face of absurdity is also what we might call success or the "joy" available to us.[5] Happiness and absurdity are linked. Struggle serves as that linkage.[6]

We must see beyond the particular task assigned Sisyphus and see the defiance in his work without reward. We are nudged to find in Sisyphus (as model) a rejection of nihilism as the final word on human effort. Camus reads the myth and finds in it a type of resistance or rebellion on the part of Sisyphus: he, for a moment, turns punishment into possibility; angst into awareness; and, repetition into resistance.

Humanism . . .

Camus offers no assurance that this happiness is indeed the case; he cannot: "One must *imagine* [emphasis added]," he proposes. Yet, we are to have sufficient lucidity—awareness, that is—to read between the lines of tradition and limitation demanded by the "gods" and instead value potential over against outcomes. Sisyphus is imagined happy not because of anything certain, but simply because there is the possibility of happiness. Sisyphus does not surrender to the absurd. There is, in his philosophical and ethical posture, his pushing, no sign of a desire to end this eternal task. The absurdity, the call of nihilism, is met and overcome through Sisyphus's continued action.

Struggle. Camus provides a new gospel of sorts, a secular epistle meant to offer symbols of possibility within a world that does not recognize such possibilities. Humanists and atheists have established something of their own icons of struggle—figures prompting an irreverent gospel of hostility and earthiness.

The New Atheists have what is commonly called—perhaps tongue in check in some cases—the "four horsemen": Richard Dawkins, Sam Harris, the late Christopher Hitchens, and Daniel Dent.[7] Their rather aggressive critique of theological considerations is meant to promote the certainties (or potentiality) of science as the basis for both public and private life. Some humanists, particularly those with a more confrontational posture toward theism(s), embrace to varying degrees the teachings of these figures. Yet, for those not in this camp, there is still an array of secular prophets (those who announce our challenges and shortcomings, while providing something of a way forward). Camus certainly should be named among them—along with Richard Wright, Lorraine Hansberry, Henry David Thoreau (though some will debate this), W. E. B. Du Bois, and so on.[8] His, Camus's, writings and insights—his political commentary and struggle—and his effort to find a way to live without God certainly shed some light on contemporary debates regarding humanist values and ethics.

The physicality of our effort to do something; the weight of our thought about being in the world, a world that does not recognize us; and the opportunity to *do* in the context of communities of the like-minded offer the humanist small comfort. We do what we can, as we can, with what we have within reach of our human grasp. In a word, "Conscious that I cannot stand aloof from my time," writes Camus, "I have decided to be an integral part of it."[9] And, he continues in a way that should spark the imagination of humanists, "I establish my lucidity in the midst of what negates it. I exalt man before what crushes him, and my freedom, my revolt, and my passion come together then in that tension, that lucidity, and that vast repetition."[10] To this, the humanist might give a godless "amen!"

By means of this voice—words and the physical mechanisms that make the agreement possible—those who share Camus's perspective express commitment to a particular moralist position. It, I argue, involves a measured realism, a confrontation with the "stuff" of life—for example, race, religion, and cultural production—without flinching and without turning away, and without Enlightenment assumptions of human progress.

Camus knew, and we should understand, history is littered with the trash of human injustice and oppression—and all this nastiness is the residue of good intentions falling victim to the trappings of power relationships and ideology replacing compassionate discourse and civil exchange. Progress inevitable? No, it is more likely that efforts toward transformation will produce misery. Camus realized this based on Second World War atrocities writ large and the dynamics of colonization in the places he knew personally; and, in the twenty-first century there are sufficient military struggles and the stench of violent death sufficient to reject the hyper-optimism of the Enlightenment. This is a different humanism, a more moderate-in-out-look humanism—one made more worldly—or world worn—based on the ways in which advances in human knowledge and capacity have worked against the flourishing of life. This awareness begs the question: how should humanists struggle to maintain dignity and Sisyphus's happiness within the context of such tragic possibilities? Freedom is a briar patch, and as the African American folktale goes, we must become like Brer Rabbit—a creative creature (a trickster of sorts who occupies the in-between spaces of existence)—and be comfortable within that rough terrain.[11]

Humanism has confronted a recent orientation in contemporary theisms. **Religion**. Nontheists are wont to claim the end of religion, and to base this on developments (or decline) in Europe. Yet, in areas of population growth—such as South America, the Middle East, and Africa, religion continues to flourish. And so many of these religious strongholds are imbued with an evangelical and dangerously conservative tone. Theism(s) continue to find audiences, despite the eulogies offered by humanists. If this were not enough to give humanists pause, the "look" of humanism in public portrays a movement that does not fully represent the racial diversity of the world. **Race**. All this takes place within the context of cultural worlds—that is, signs, symbols, narratives, practices, and the aesthetics of human effort to trace the world—humanists may not understand in an adequate fashion. **Cultural production**. With respect to cultural trends, humanists may constitute the odd uncle who is out of the loop, and only reluctantly included in family activities. Humanism's predicament, as I understand it, takes places within an evolving context marked by great potential and by an equally energetic possibility of loss. Again, race, religion, and culture demand attention—organized, layered, and flexible enough to recognize historical shifts. And, it must be done in such a way as to hold in check ego—assumptions that "we" handle these issues well because we do not abide by superstitions that justify nonsense. In light of the chapters in this volume, I propose that humanists give attention to the challenge posed by the three from an important but somewhat marginal perspective.

EPILOGUE: SISYPHUS'S HAPPINESS

1. Religion is not going away, despite the projections to the contrary offered by nontheists. And of great importance, there is a distinction to be made between religion and theism;

2. Much of the conversation within humanist circles is Eurocentric and presumes race a problem to solve as opposed to a necessity that has the potential to transform humanist communities for the best. This involves, however, humanists being willing to view humanism from the perspective of racial difference.

3. Marginal modalities of cultural production such as hip-hop culture hold great possibility for helping humanism to advance—for example, rebrand and develop organic strategies.

Struggle to make a difference in the world, for the humanist, has no guaranteed outcomes; but instead, humanists gain some sense of living through the mere fact that they can struggle, can do . . . something despite what that doing may or may not achieve. Race, religion, and the dynamics of cultural production are three of the challenges confronting humanists in their doing.

Stated one last time, they, these three, in a particular way, constitute something of the rock the humanist works indefinitely to move. The task is to address this rock—the challenge of three—in such a way as to be able to imagine oneself (and be imagined) happy.

Notes

Introduction

1 Albert Camus, *The Myth of Sisyphus and Other Essays* (New York: Vintage International, 1991), 119–20.

2 Alain de Botton, *Religion for Atheists: A Non-Believer's Guide to the Uses of Religion* (New York: Vintage, 2013).

3 Anthony B. Pinn, *The End of God-Talk: An African American Humanist Theology* (New York: Oxford University Press, 2012), 149–50.

4 William R. Jones, *Is God a White Racist? A Preamble to Black Theology* (Boston: Beacon Press, 1997); Norm Allen, *African American Humanism: An Anthology* (Buffalo, NY: Prometheus, 1991); Allen, *The Black Humanist Experience: An Alternative to Religion* (Buffalo, NY: Prometheus, 2002); Michael Lackey, *African American Atheists and Political Liberation: A Study of the Sociocultural Dynamics of Faith* (Gainesville, FL: University Press of Florida, 2008); Sikivu Hutchinson, *Moral Combat: Black Atheists, Gender Politics, and the Values War* (Los Angeles: Infidel Books, 2011); Hutchinson, *Godless Americana: Race and Religious Rebels* (Los Angeles: Infidel Books, 2013); Anthony Pinn, *Why, Lord? Suffering and Evil in Black Theology* (New York: Continuum, 1995); Pinn, *By These Hands: A Documentary History of African American Humanism* (New York: New York University Press, 2001); Pinn, *African American Humanist Principles: Living and Thinking Like the Children of Nimrod* (New York: Palgrave Macmillan, 2004); Pinn, *The End of God-Talk*, 2012; and Pinn, *What Has the Black Church to Do With Public Life?* (New York: Palgrave Macmillan, 2013).

5 Alain de Botton, *Religion for Atheists: A Non-Believer's Guide to the Uses of Religion* (New York: Vintage, 2012); Greg Epstein, *Good Without God: What a Billion Nonreligious People Do Believe* (New York: William Morrow Paperbacks, Reissue Edition, 2010). One should also take note of the work of A. C. Grayling. Such as: Grayling, *Meditations for the Humanist: Ethics for a Secular Age* (New York: Oxford University Press, 2003); Grayling, *The Good Book: A Humanist Bible*, Reprinted Edition (London: Walker & Company, 2013). There is also Grayling's *The God Argument: The Case Against Religion and for Humanism* (New York: Bloomsbury USA, 2013).

Chapter one

1. This chapter is a modified version of "African American Humanism in Practice and Thought," in Miguel De La Torre (ed.), *The Hope of Liberation in the World Religions* (Waco, TX: Baylor University Press, 2008), 51–64.
2. Although African American humanist orientations are not accurately understood as a simple outgrowth of Enlightenment-based theologies, because their existential sensibilities emerge within a context of oppression generated within the modern period's political-economic and cultural developments, some of their vocabulary and grammar is drawn (both explicitly and implicitly) from earlier modalities of liberal theologies framed by the Enlightenment.
3. Jones, *Is God a White Racist?*, 1997.
4. Henry David Thoreau, *Walden* (Princeton: Princeton University Press, 1979).
5. Pinn, *Why, Lord?*, ch. 6.
6. Pinn, *Why, Lord?*, 1995.
7. Robert L. Pope, "'The Tendency of Modern Theology,' *AME Church Review* 27 (April 11)," in Stephen Angell and Anthony B. Pinn (eds), *Social Protest Thought in the African Methodist Episcopal Churchy, 1862-1939* (Knoxville: The University of Tennessee Press, 2000), 133.
8. Norman W. Brown, "'What the Negro Thinks of God,' *AME Church Review* 51 (April–June 1935)," in Stephen Angell and Anthony B. Pinn (eds), *Social Protest Thought in the African Methodist Episcopal Churchy, 1862-1939* (Knoxville: The University of Tennessee Press, 2000), 137.
9. Brown, *Social Protest Thought in the African Methodist Episcopal Churchy, 1862-1939*, 138.
10. This dichotomy also becomes a way of distinguishing clearly theistic forms of African American religion ("other-worldly") from more humanistic strands ("this-worldly"). For a good introduction to this debate see: Gayraud Wilmore, *Black Religion and Black Radicalism: An Interpretation of the Religious History of Afro-American People* (Garden City, NY: Doubleday, 1972; 2nd edn, Maryknoll, NY: Orbis Books, 1983).
11. Anthony B. Pinn, *The Black Church in the Post-Civil Rights Era* (Maryknoll, NY: Orbis Books, 2002), 17–18.
12. The number of scholarly treatments of the Megachurch phenomenon is increasing. See as examples of this development: Shaynee Lee, *T. D. Jakes: Americas New Preacher* (New York: New York University Press, 2005); Milmon F. Harrison, *Righteous Riches: The Word of Faith Movement in Contemporary African American Religion* (New York: Oxford University Press, 2005).
13. Martin L. King, Jr, "How should a Christian view Communism?," in *Strength to Love* (Philadelphia: Fortress Press, 1963), 101.
14. Daniel Payne, "Daniel Payne's Protestation of Slavery," in *Lutheran Herald and Journal of the Franckean Synod* (Fort Plain: NY: Committee of Publication of the Franckean Synod, 1839), 115.

15 Although it is possible that Christianity was replaced by another theistic orientation in the life of this young man, it remains clear that he brings into question certain modalities of Christian expression and, in this way, supports modalities of humanism (whether theistic or not).

16 "Experiences of a Chimney Sweeper," in J. Mason Brewer (ed.), *America's Negro Folklore* (Chicago: Quadrangle Books, 1968), 268.

17 Here and elsewhere I understand religion to mean the quest for complex subjectivity, and theology is the exploration (celebration and critique) of this quest. For more information on this theory of religion see: Anthony B. Pinn, *Terror and Triumph: The Nature of Black Religion* (Minneapolis: Fortress Press, 2003).

18 For examples of this see: James Forman, *The Making of Black Revolutionaries* (Washington, DC: Open Hand Publishing, 1985); Toni Morrison (ed.), *To Die for the People: The Writings of Huey P. Newton*, reprint edn (New York: Writers and Readers Publishing, Inc., 1995).

19 Richard Wright, *The Outsider*, Library of America Edition (New York: HareperPerennial, 1991). Also see Richard Wright, *Black Boy*, Library of America Edition (New York: HarperPerennial, 1991); See Anthony B. Pinn, *African American Humanist Principles: Living and Thinking Like the Children of Nimrod* (New York: Palgrave Macmillan, 2005); Pinn, *By These Hands*, 2001; Norm Allen, Jr, *African American Humanism: An Anthology* (Buffalo, NY: Prometheus Books, 1991).

20 Quoted in Pinn, *African American Humanist Principles*, 19.

21 As readers might assume, for African American members of the UUA, the above call for justice is given a concrete context in which issues of racism are given significance. It was this demand for explicit attention to racism as a requirement for justice (or what is called liberation in other contexts) that marked the greatest period of stress within the UUA, when African Americans in the 1970s called for greater participation in the pressing sociopolitical drama of the United States through a purging of the Association's own racism. See *Empowerment: One Denomination's Quest for Racial Justice, 1967-1982* (Boston: Unitarian Universalist Association, 1993).

22 http://www.uua.org/aboutuua/principles.html.

23 http://www.uua.org/.

Chapter two

1 This essay was first published as "Living Life: African Americans and Humanism," in "The Colors of Humanism," a special issue of *Essays in the Philosophy of Humanism*, 20, 1 (June 2012): 23–30.

2 Cornel West, *Prophesy Deliverance! An Afro-American Revolutionary Christianity* (Philadelphia: Westminster John Knox, 1982), 44.

3 W. E. B. Du Bois, *The Souls of Black Folk* (New York: Vintage Books, 1990), 8.

4 Richard Wright, *Black Boy* (New York: Harper & Row, Publishers, 1966), 123–4.
5 Frederick Douglass, *Narrative of the Life of Frederick Douglass* (1845).
6 "American Religious Identification Survey 2008: http://b27.cc.trincoll.edu/weblogs/AmericanReligionSurvey-ARIS/reports/p3a_race.html.
7 http://www.facebook.com/group.php?gid=162810514308&v=wall.
8 See for example: Peter Steinfels, "Scandinavian Nonbelievers, Which Is Not to Say Atheists," *New York Times*: http://www.nytimes.com/2009/02/28/us/28beliefs.html.
9 A portion of this paragraph is drawn from Anthony B. Pinn, " Remembering African American Humanism," http://www.americanhumanist.org/HNN/details/2011-02-remembering-african-american-humanism.

Chapter three

1 First posted on the Richard Dawkins Foundation website (May 4, 2012). See: "Do Atheist Understand and Appreciate Black Bodies?" http://old.richarddawkins.net/articles/645837-do-atheists-understand-and-appreciate-black-bodies.
2 http://topics.nytimes.com/top/reference/timestopics/people/m/trayvon_martin/index.html.
3 I develop this idea more fully in: Pinn, *African American Humanist Principles: Living and Thinking Like the Children of Nimrod* (Palgrave, 2004) and *The End of God-Talk: An African American Humanist Theology* (Oxford, 2012). While the historical and cultural context for these texts are clearly African American, the basic principles outlined are easily relevant to other communities as well.
4 Michelle Alexander, *The New Jim Crow* (New York: The New Press, 2011).

Chapter four

1 This chapter was first published as a Review Essay of *W. E. B. Du Bois: An American Prophet* by Edward Blum, *Divine Discontent* by Jonathon Kahn and *Tragic Soul-Life* by Terrence Johnson, *The Journal of Religion* (July 2014). The version here is slightly expanded.
2 All references are to these texts: Edward J. Blum, *W. E. B. Du Bois: American Prophet*. (Philadelphia, PA: University of Pennsylvania Press, 2007); Jonathon S. Kahn, *Divine Discontent: The Religious Imagination of W. E. B. Du Bois* (New York: Oxford University Press, 2009); Terrence L. Johnson, *Tragic Soul-Life: W. E. B. Du Bois and the Moral Crisis Facing American Democracy* (New York: Oxford University Press, 2012); W. E. B. Du Bois, *The Souls of Black Folk* (New York: Penguin Books, 1996).

3   See for example: James Cone and Gayraud Wilmore, *Black Theology: A Documentary History, Volumes 1-2* (Maryknoll, NY: Orbis Books, 1991).

4   Howard Thurman, *Jesus and the Disinherited* (Richmond, IN: Friends United Press, 2000); Dietrich Bonheoffer, *Letters from Prison* (Maryknoll, NY: Orbis Books, 2002).

5   For an example of how Pragmatism informs African American religion, see Cornel West, *Prophesy Deliverance* (Louisville: Westminster/John Knox, 1982).

6   Johnson's book appears in the series I coedited with Caroline Levander, "Imagining the Americas."

7   It was this nontraditional take on and response to religion that troubled Joseph Washington: "To their peril, some have attempted to use Black Religion for their own designs and separate its concern about the Ultimate from its ultimate concern.... W. E. B. Du Bois tried it, to his peril." Joseph R. Washington, Jr, "The Peculiar Peril and Promise of Black Folk Religion," in David Edwin Harrell, Jr (ed.), *Varieties of Southern Evangelicalism* (Macon, GA: Mercer University Press, 1981), 68.

8   Gerald Horne, *Black and Red* (Albany: State University of New York Press, 1986), 16. This is taken from Du Bois to B. P. Moreno, November 15, 1948, Reel 62, #381, Du Bois Papers, University of Massachusetts, Amherst.

9   See Phil Zuckerman (ed.). *Du Bois on Religion* (Lanham: Altamira, 2000); Jonathan Kahn, "Religion and the Political Vision of W. E. B. Du Bois," PhD Dissertation, Columbia University, 2003.

10 Interesting discussions of Du Bois and the religious include: Jonathon S. Kahn, *Divine Discontent: The Religious Imagination of W. E. B. Du Bois* (New York: Oxford University Press, 2009); Edward J. Blum, *W. E. B. Du Bois: American Prophet* (Philadelphia: University of Pennsylvania Press, 2007). Both seek to rethink what has been a rather quick dismissal of Du Bois as engaged with the "religious" in his work/life.

11 http://www.negrospirituals.com/news-song/children_go_where_i_sens_thee.htm.

Chapter five

1   This chapter combines two pieces: "God of Restraint: An African American Humanist Interpretation of Nimrod and the Tower of Babel," in Anthony B. Pinn and Allen D. Callahan (eds), *African American Religious Life and the Story of Nimrod* (New York: Palgrave Macmillan, 2007), 26–34; and "God's Obituary: A Humanist Response to Mass Murder," *Religion Dispatches* (December 25, 2012). See: http://www.religiondispatches.org/archive/atheologies/6702/god_s_obituary__a_humanist_response_to_mass_murder.

2   Pinn, *African American Humanist Principles*, 6.

3   Genesis 3:22-24 (King James Version). I would not argue that the serpent who plays a role in "original sin" was good. No, whereas God as restraint seeks to

prevent human freedom to safeguard certain relationships we assume good, the serpent seeks to open them for their problematic possibilities: radical good versus radical evil. Neither is beneficial.

4 Genesis 9:25 (King James Version).
5 Genesis 11:4-6 (King James Version).
6 A similar argument is made in "The Hypostasis of the Archons," found in the Nag Hammadi Library. In this account, an effort is made to keep "Adam" in ignorance. The "rulers" are presented as acting against the interest of humans by attempting to restrict knowledge. I am grateful to Allen Callahan, my coeditor, for bringing this account to my attention.
7 Genesis 3:22-24 (King James Version).
8 For an interesting interpretation of the story of Babel that takes up this question of God's intent but offers an alternate, one that justifies God's actions, see: Leon R. Kass, "What's Wrong With Babel?," in Georgy Wolfe (ed.), *The New Religious Humanists: A Reader* (New York: The Free Press, 1997), 60–83.
9 Frank Burch Brown, *Religious Aesthetics: A Theological Study of Making and Meaning* (Princeton: Princeton University Press, 2004), 131–2.
10 Genesis 11:6-8 (King James Version).

Chapter six

1 This chapter was first published as, "Thoughts on Martin Luther King, Jr.'s God, Humanist Sensibilities, and Moral Evil," *Theology Today*, 65, 1 (April 2008): 57–66.
2 Particularly Pinn, *Why, Lord?*, 1995; Pinn, *Varieties of African American Religious Experience* (Minneapolis: Fortress Press), 198; Pinn (ed.), *Moral Evil and Redemptive Suffering: A Documentary History* (Gainesville, FL: University Press of Florida, 2001).
3 Particularly as presented in *African American Humanist Principles: Living and Thinking Like the Children of Nimrod* (New York: Palgrave Macmillan, 2004).
4 I imagine there is little doubt such is the case with King. However, for work on how this is also true for African American Humanism see Pinn (ed.), *By These Hands*, 2001. Furthermore, it should be noted that I am not offering a full description of King's thought and its genesis. I am not a King scholar, but rather one who studies African American religious thought and religiosity from a variety of angles and through some attention to a variety of figures. A more "authoritative" take on King's intellectual formulation is the task of others working on a different type of project.
5 Martin L. King, Jr, *Where Do We Go From Here: Chaos or Community* (Boston: Beacon Press, 1968), 123.
6 Martin L. King, Jr, "The Case Against 'Tokenism'," in James Washington (ed.), *A Testament of Hope: The Essential Writings of Martin Luther King, Jr.*, (New York: HarperCollins, 1986), 108.

7 Rufus Burrows, *God and Human Dignity: The Personalism, Theology, and Ethics of Martin Luther King, Jr.* (Notre Dame: University of Notre Dame Press, 2006), 99–100.
8 Burrows, *God and Human Dignity*, 101.
9 Burrows, *God and Human Dignity*, 106, 111–13.
10 Rufus Burrows, "Personalism, the Objective Moral Order, and Moral Law in the Work of Martin Luther King, Jr.", in Lewis V. Baldwin et al., *The Legacy of Martin Luther King, Jr.: The Boundaries of Law, Politics, and Religion* (Notre Dame, IN: University of Notre Dame Press, 2002), 220–1.
11 Delores Williams, *Sisters in the Wilderness* (Maryknoll, NY: Orbis Books, 1993).
12 Kelly Brown Douglas, *What's Faith Got to Do With It? Black Bodies/Christian Souls* (Maryknoll, NY: Orbis Books, 2005), 96.
13 Douglas, *What's Faith Got to Do With It?*, 100.
14 See for example: Thomas J. J. Altizer and William Hamilton, *Radical Theology and the Death of God* (New York: The Bobbs-Merrill Company, Inc., 1966).
15 Howard Thurman probably comes closest within African American thought to this ideal relationship between God and world, but even he recognizes the manner in which racism, for instance, blocks our ability to achieve such the blurring of boundaries of self in all.

Chapter seven

1 This chapter first appeared as "Looking for Me? Jesus Images, Christology, and the Limitations of Theological Blackness," in George Yancy (ed.), *Christology and Whiteness* (New York: Routledge, 2012), 453–70.
2 Stephen Prothero, *American Jesus: How the Son of God Became a National Icon* (New York: Farrar, Straus and Giroux, 2003), 13.
3 Prothero, *American Jesus*, 14.
4 David Morgan, *The Sacred Gaze: Religious Visual Culture in Theory and Practice* (Berkeley: University of California Press, 2005), 247–55.
5 "More Like Jesus Would I Be," http://www.hymnlyrics.org/lyricsm/more_like_jesus_would_I_be.html (Viewed March 23, 2011).
6 Morgan, *The Sacred Gaze*, 248–9.
7 David Morgan, *Visual Piety: A History and Theory of Popular Religious Images* (Berkeley: University of California Press, 1998), 17.
8 Morgan, *Visual Piety*, 18.
9 Morgan, *Visual Piety*, 123.
10 Morgan, *Visual Piety*, 123.
11 Orlando Patterson, *Slavery and Social Death: A Comparative Study* (Cambridge: Harvard University Press, 1985).

12. "There Is a Balm in Gilead," http://www.negrospirituals.com/news-song/there_is_a_blam_in_gilead.htm (Viewed on March 21, 2011).
13. "Ride on King Jesus," http://www.negrospirituals.com/news-song/ride_on_king_jesus.htm (Viewed on March 21, 2011).
14. "Nobody Knows De Trouble I've Had," http://www.negrospirituals.com/news-song/nobody_knows_de_trouble_i.htm (Viewed on March 21, 2011).
15. "Buked and Scorned," http://www.negrospirituals.com/news-song/buked_and_scorned.htm (Viewed on March 21, 2011).
16. Wilson Moses, *The Wings of Ethiopia: Studies in African-American Life and Letters* (Ames: Iowa University Press, 1990), 168.
17. Isaiah 53:5 (English Standard Version).
18. Anthony B. Pinn, *Moral Evil and Redemptive Suffering: A History of Theodicy in African-American Religious Thought* (Gainesville: University Press of Florida, 2002), 132–3.
19. James Theodore Holly, "The Divine Plan of Human Redemption in Its Ethnological Development," in Anthony B. Pinn (ed.), *Moral Evil and Redemptive Suffering: A History of Theodicy in African-American Religious Thought* (Gainesville: University Press of Florida, 2002), 139.
20. Stephen Protero provides attention to some of the more apparent examples of this process in "Black Moses," in *American Jesus: How the Son of God Became a National Icon* (New York: Farrar, Straus and Giroux, 2003), 200–28.
21. Kelly Brown Douglas, *The Black Christ* (New York: Orbis Books, 1994), 1.
22. James H. Cone, *A Black Theology of Liberation*, 20th Anniversary edn (Maryknoll, NY: Orbis Books, 1986), ch. 4.
23. Cone, *A Black Theology of Liberation*, 111.
24. Cone, *A Black Theology of Liberation*, 121.
25. James H. Cone, *God of the Oppressed* (New York: Harper & Row, Publishers, 1975), 134.
26. Some of the following discussion of Black Jesus is drawn from an early version of chapter six in Anthony B. Pinn, *Embodiment and the New Shape of Black Theological Thought* (New York: New York University Press, 2009).
27. In Rob Marriott, "Last Testament," *Vibe Magazine* (November 1996): T7.
28. Tupac Shakur, "Blasphemy," *The Don Killuminati, The 7 Day Theory* (Interscope Records, 1996).
29. Jacquelyn Grant, *White Women's Christ and Black Women's Jesus: Feminist Christology and Womanist Response* (Atlanta: Scholars Press, 1989), 213.
30. Kelly Brown Douglas, *The Black Christ* (Maryknoll, NY: Orbis Books, 1994), 85–6.
31. Douglas, *The Black Christ*, 108–9.
32. Wilson Jeremiah Moses, *Black Messiahs and Uncle Toms: Social and Literary Manipulations of a Religious Myth* (University Park: The Pennsylvania State University Press, 1982), x–xi.

33 Rene Girard, *Violence and the Sacred* (Baltimore: Johns Hopkins University Press, 1977).

34 Girard, *Violence and the Sacred*, trans. Patrick Gregory, 1977; Delores Williams, *Sisters in the Wilderness* (Maryknoll, NY: Orbis Books, 1993).

35 Luther H. Martin, Huck Gutman, and Patrick H. Hutton (eds), *Technologies of the Self: A Seminar with Michel Foucault* (Amherst: The University of Massachusetts Press, 1988), 22.

36 Erving Goffman, *Stigma: Notes on the Management of Spoiled Identity* (New York: Simon & Schuster, 1963).

37 Goffman, *Stigma*, 6.

38 Adopting Victor Anderson's sense of this as "a species logic in which every individual member of a species shares essential traits that identify the member within the species." See Anderson, *Beyond Ontological Blackness* (New York: Continuum, 1995), 51.

39 I first make this argument in *Why, Lord? Suffering and Evil in Black Theology* (New York: Continuum, 1995).

40 Erving Goffman, "The Stigmatized Self," in Charles Lemert and Ann Branaman (eds), *The Goffman Reader* (Malden, MA: Blackwell Publishers, 1997), 73.

41 Ann Branaman, "Goffman's Social Theory," in Charles Lemert and Ann Branaman (eds), *The Goffman Reader* (Malden, MA: Blackwell Publishers, 1997), xlvii.

42 Victor Anderson, *Beyond Ontological Blackness* (New York: Continuum, 1995), 91–2.

43 Anderson, *Beyond Ontological Blackness*, 92–3.

44 Nikki Sullivan, *Tattooed Bodies: Subjectivity, Textuality, Ethics, and Pleasure* (Westport, CT: Praeger, 2001), 2.

45 Alec McHoul and Wendy Grace, *A Foucault Primer: Discourse, Power and the Subject* (New York: New York University Press, 1993), 41.

46 This phrasing is drawn from Victor Anderson, *Beyond Ontological Blackness* (New York: Continuum, 1995), 61, 78.

47 This is from Pinn, *Embodiment and the New Shape of Black Theological Thought*, 2009.

48 Jeremy R. Carrette, *Foucault and Religion: Spiritual Corporality and Political Spirituality* (New York: Routledge, 2000), 112–13.

49 Susan Bordo, "'Material Girl': The Effacements of Postmodern Culture," in Donn Welton (ed.), *Body and Flesh: A Philosophical Reader* (Malden, MA: Blackwell Publishers, Inc., 1998), 89, 91.

Chapter eight

1 Matthew 18:20 (New International Version).

2 Acts 1:12-16 (New International Version).

3 Numerous articles and books have been produced in recent years which are meant to address this concern for community and ritualization of life. See, for example, Dale McGowan and Anthony Pinn (eds), *Everyday Humanism* (Equinox, 2014).

4 See Pinn (ed.), *Theism and Public Policy: Humanist Responses* (New York: Palgrave Macmillan, 2014).

5 I discuss this in terms of black churches, as a case study, in Pinn, *What Has the Black Church to Do With Public Life?* (New York: Palgrave Macmillan, 2013).

6 For an interesting and brief discussion of increased interest in this area of study see: Elisabeth Arweck, Stephen Bullivant, and Lois Lee (eds), *Secularity and Non-Religion* (London: Routledge, 2014), ch. 1.

7 Jonathan A. Laman, "The Importance of Religious Displays for Belief Acquisition and Secularization," in Elisabeth Arweck, Stephen Bullivant, and Lois Lee (eds), *Secularity and Non-Religion* (London: Routledge, 2014), 31–47.

8 Anthony Pinn, *Terror and Triumph: The Nature of Black Religion* (Minneapolis: Fortress Press, 2002); Pinn, *The End of God-Talk: An African American Humanist Theology* (New York: Oxford University Press, 2012).

9 For additional information on my defining of religion see: Pinn, *Terror and Triumph*; and Pinn, *The End of God-Talk*. While in these books I have framed this understanding of religion in terms of African Americans, it is not a theorization of religion necessarily restricted to African Americans. I use the African American context as a case study of sorts.

10 Stephen Eric Bronner, *Camus: Portrait of a Moralist* (Chicago: University of Chicago Press, 2009), 12–14.

11 Colin Campbell, *Toward Sociology of Irreligion* (New York: Herder and Herder, 1972), 21.

12 Campbell, *Toward Sociology of Irreligion*, 25.

13 An early example of this would include, Campbell, *Toward a Sociology of Irreligion*, ch. 1.

14 The volume below is based on a central question. Contributors were asked to predict the "place" of religion within the next half century. The discussion of secularity in both Europe and the United States may be of interest to readers: Grace David, Pau Heelas, and Linda Woodhead (eds), *Predicting Religion: Christian, Secular and Alternative Futures* (Burlington, VT: Ashgate Publishing Company, 2003). It is important to note that by community I mean particular configurations of human connection that can be localized or virtual, but that foster a particular bond based on shared sensibilities and outlooks. This differs from my use of the term in my humanist theology. See, Pinn, *The End of God-Talk*, ch. 2.

15 For the European context, see for instance, Kate Hunt, "Understanding the Spirituality of People Who Do Not Go to Church," in *Predicting Religion*, 159–69.

16 www.uua.org/documents/uua/140212_uua_brand_story (Accessed on June 7, 2014).

17 See: http://www.uua.org/beliefs/congregationallife/worship/ (Accessed on June 7, 2014).

NOTES

18 http://nyc.sundayassembly.com/about/ (Accessed June 9, 2014).
19 http://nyc.sundayassembly.com/about/ (Accessed June 9, 2014).
20 http://nyc.sundayassembly.com/about/ (Accessed March 24, 2014).
21 http://sundayassembly.com/story/ (Accessed March 24, 2014).
22 http://www.vice.com/print/no-god-no-problem-0000206-v21n1 (Accessed March 24, 2014).
23 http://www.theguardian.com/commentisfree/andrewbrown/2013 (Accessed March 24, 2014).
24 http://www.religiondispatches.org/archive/atheologies/7356/uk (Accessed March 24, 2014).
25 http://sundayassembly.com/story/ (Accessed March 24, 2014).
26 http://sundayassembly.com/public-charter-for-the-sunday-assembly/ (Accessed March 24, 2014).
27 http://religiondispatches.org/archive/atheologies/7498/are (Accessed January 14, 2014).
28 What I present here is not based on interviews, but rather it draws strictly from observation. My reason for this approach revolves around my concern to approach this discussion based on how those unfamiliar with these gatherings might encounter them. To hold interviews and use that information would move the discussion in the direction of intent, rather than focusing on the dynamics of experience.
29 See: http://video.msnbc.msn.com/up/46848396#46848396; http://www.youtube.com/watch?v=CgZlkYuJQCU (Accessed on June 9, 2014).
30 http://www.houstonoasis.org/wp/about/ (Accessed January 10, 2014).
31 http://www.houstonoasis.org/wp/about/ (Accessed January 10, 2014).
32 http://www.houstonoasis.org/wp/about/ (Accessed January 10, 2014).
33 Alain de Botton's godless uses of religion and accompanying practices merit consideration in this regard, but that is for a different project. I have in mind his "School of Life," which is concerned with offering people information and activities that enhance living. Rather than a church model, it is based on structures of educational exchange—e.g., schools—through classes. Still, even it draws from church language and practices; such is the case with its "secular sermons."
34 Greg Epstein, *Good Without God: What a Billion Nonreligious People Do Believe* (New York: William Morrow Paperbacks, 2010), ch. 6.
35 See, for instance: http://www.christianpost.com/news/richard-dawkins-i-guess-im-a-cultural-christian-91312/. This idea is addressed as well in Greg Epstein's book: *Good Without God: What a Billion Nonreligious People Do Believe* (New York: William Morrow Paperbacks, 2010), ch. 6.
36 I take up some of these issues in Pinn, *The End of God-Talk*, ch. 6.
37 This paragraph is drawn from "Watch the Body With New Eyes: Womanist Thought's Contribution to a Humanist Notion of Ritual," *CrossCurrents*, 57, 3 (Fall 2007): 404–11.

Chapter nine

1 This essay combines "Can Atheist Billboards Kill Religion?" Religion Dispatches (May 1, 2012); "Atheists Gathering in Burbank: A Humanist Perspective" Religion Dispatches (October 27, 2009); and, "Thoughts on What Humanists Might Learn from Hip Hop," *Free Inquiry*, 32, 6 (October/November 2011–12): 31–5. See: http://www.religiondispatches.org/archive/atheologies/5823/can_atheist_billboards_kill_religion; and http://www.religiondispatches.org/archive/atheologies/1894/atheists_gather_in_burbank__a_humanist_s_response.
2 Jones, *Is God a White Racist?*, 1996.
3 Hebrews 11:1.
4 Attention to the ordinary presented here draws from the *End of God-Talk: An African American Humanist Theology* (New York: Oxford University Press, 2012).
5 Some material in this section draws from the discussion of perpetual rebellion found in *Terror and Triumph: The Nature of Black Religion* (Minneapolis: Fortress Press, 2003), 153–4.
6 Sharon Welch, *A Feminist Ethic of Risk* (Minneapolis: Fortress Press, 2000).
7 Michel Foucault, *Ethics: Subjectivity and Truth*, ed. Paul Rabinow (New York: The New Press, 1997), 319.

Chapter ten

1 This article is one of four on death that I have recently developed. All draw, to differing degrees, from Albert Camus and rap music; but they address different dimensions of the question of death. The others include "Zombies in the 'Hood: Rap Music, Camusian Absurdity, and the Structuring of Death," in Monica Miller and Anthony B. Pinn (eds), *Religion in Hip Hop: The New Terrain* (London: Bloomsbury Academic), forthcoming; and, "The End: Thoughts on Humanism and Death," for inclusion in a special issue of the journal *Dialog*.
2 W. E. B. Du Bois, "On the Passing of the First-Born," *The Souls of Black Folk* (Mineola, NY: Dover Publications, 1994).
3 See for instance: http://www.youtube.com/watch?v=h4ZyuULy9zs (Accessed on January 31, 2014). For a history of the song, readers should consider David Margolick's *Strange Fruit: The Biography of a Song* (New York: Harper Perennial, 2001).
4 Interesting work on Robert Johnson includes Peter Guralnick's *Searching for Robert Johnson: The Life and Legend of the "King of the Delta Blues Singers"* (New York: Plume, 1998).

5 Philip A. Mellor, "Death in high modernity: The contemporary presence and absence of death," in David Clark (ed.), *The Sociology of Death* (Cambridge, MA: Blackwell Publishers, 1993), 11–12.

6 Allan Kellehear, *A Social History of Dying* (London: Cambridge University Press, 2007), 47.

7 Genesis 3: 17-19 (New International Version).

8 David Clark, "Introduction," *The Sociology of Death* (Cambridge, MA: Blackwell Publishers, 1993), 3.

9 Albert Camus, "The Renegade, or a Confused Mind," in *Exile and the Kingdom* (New York: Vintage International, 2007); Tupac Shakur, *The Don Killuminati: The 7Day Theory* (Los Angeles: Death Row/Interscope 1996); Albert Camus, *The Rebel* (New York: Vintage International, 1991), 297, 300–1.

10 Tupac Shakur, "Blasphemy," in *The Don Killuminati: The 7 Day Theory* (Los Angeles: Death Row Records, 1996).

11 Shakur, "Blasphemy," 1996.

12 Shakur, "Blasphemy," 1996.

13 Camus, *The Rebel*, 55; Shakur, "Blasphemy," 1996.

14 Tupac Shakur, "All Eyez on Me," in *All Eyez on Me* (Los Angeles: Death Row/Interscope, 1996).

15 Thug Life, "The Hate U Give Little Infants Fucks Everybody"; Tupac Shakur, "Only God Can Judge Me," *All Eyez on Me* (Los Angeles: Death Row/Interscope, 1996); Jay Z, "Moment of Clarity," *The Black Album* (New York Roc-A-Fella/Def Jam, 2003).

16 Camus, *The Rebel*, 24–5.

17 For example: http://www.donmega.com/20-reasons-why-tupac-is-still-alive.php (Accessed January 31, 2014).

18 Shakur, "Blasphemy," 1996.

19 Camus, *The Rebel*, 23.

20 Corinthians 15:55 (New International Version).

21 See, http://www.theplace2.ru/archive/tupac_shakur/img/12-35.jpg (Accessed on January 31, 2014).

22 Tupac Shakur, "Hail Mary," *Makaveli: The Don Killuminati, the 7-day theory* (Los Angeles: Death Row Records, 1996).

23 Camus, *The Rebel*, 55; Shakur, "Blasphemy," 1996.

24 Jay Z and Kanye West, "No Church in the Wild," *Watch the Throne* (New York: Roc-A-Fella Records, 2011).

25 Jay Z and West, "No Church in the Wild," 2011.

26 Jay Z and West, "No Church in the Wild," 2012.

27 Jay Z and Kanye West, "Who Gon Stop Me," *Watch the Throne* (New York: Roc-A-Fella Records, 2011); Camus, *The Rebel*, 1991.

28 Michel de Montaigne, "That To Study Philosophy Is to Learn to Die," in Montaigne (ed.), The Essays of Montaigne. See Gutenberg Project: http://www.gutenberg.org/files/3600/3600-h/3600-h.htm (Accessed on June 25, 2014).

29 Jay Z and Kanye West, "Niggas in Paris," *Watch the Throne* (New York: Roc-A-Fella Records, 2012).

30 Jay Z and West, "Who Gon Stop Me," 2011; Jay Z, "F.U.T.W." *Magna Carta* (New York: Roc-A-Fello Records, 2013).

31 Jay Z and West, "No Church in the Wild," 2012.

32 Richard Wright, "The Man Who Lived Underground," in *Eight Men* (New York: HarperPerennial, 1996), 30. For more of my analysis of this story, see Pinn, *The End of God-Talk*, 2012, ch. 4. Chapter 3 will be of interest as well.

33 http://rapgenius.com/Grandmaster-flash-and-the-furious-five-the-message-lyrics (Accessed June 25, 2014).

Chapter eleven

1 This essay combines the following pieces: "Naming What We Want: Thoughts on Religious Vocabulary and the Desire for Quality of Life," in Mary Fulkerson and Rosemary Carbine (eds), *Theological Perspectives on Life, Liberty and the Pursuit of Happiness* (New York: Palgrave Macmillan, 2013), 101–8; "Politics and the Limits of Religious Optimism," *Tikkun Magazine*, October 25, 2012, http://www.tikkun.org/nextgen/politics-and-the-limits-of-religious-optimism; and several pieces from Religion Dispatches.

2 See, for instance, Mathew Avery Sutton, *Jerry Falwell and the Rise of the Religious Right: A Brief History with Documents* (New York: St. Martins, 2012); Richard Crouter, *Reinhold Niebuhr: On Politics, Religion, and Christian Faith* (New York: Oxford University Press, 2010).

3 Michael Shermer, *The Believing Brain: From Ghosts and Gods to Politics and Conspiracies – How We Construct Beliefs and Reinforce Them as Truths* (New York: St. Martins, 2011).

4 Benedict Anderson, *Imagined Communities: Reflections on the Origin and Spread of Nationalism*, rev. edn. (New York: Verso, 1983).

5 David J. Linden, *The Compass of Pleasure: How Our Brains Make Fatty Foods, Orgasm, Exercise, Marijuana, Generosity, Vodka, Learning, and Gambling Feel So Good* (New York: Penguin Books, 2011).

6 Religion Dispatches: http://religiondispatches.org/.

Epilogue

1 Albert Camus, *Notebooks 1935-1942* (New York: Vintage International, 1991).

2 Albert Camus, *The Myth of Sisyphus and Other Essays* (New York: Vintage International, 1991), 102.

3 Camus, *The Myth of Sisyphus and Other Essays*, 119.

4 Camus, *The Myth of Sisyphus and Other Essays*, 120–1.

5 Camus, *The Myth of Sisyphus and Other Essays*, 120, 121–2.

6 Camus, *The Myth of Sisyphus and Other Essays*, 122.

7 Books include: Richard Dawkins, *The God Delusion*, rep. edn (New York: Mariner Books, 2008); Sam Harris, *The End of Faith: Religion, Terror, and the Future of Reason*, rep. edn (New York: W. W. Norton, 2005); Christopher Hitchens, *God Is Not Great: How Religion Poisons Everything* (New York: Twelve, 2009); Daniel Dennett, *Breaking the Spell: Religion as a Natural Phenomenon*, rep. edn (New York: Penguin Books, 2007).

8 I have in mind texts such as: Richard Wright, *Black Boy* (New York: Harper Perennial Modern Classics, 2007); Lorraine Hansberry, "A Raisin in the Sun" (New York: Vintage, 2004); Henry David Thoreau, *Walden* (Princeton: Princeton University Press, 1970); W. E. B. Du Bois, *Dusk of Dawn*, 1st edn (New York: Oxford University Press, 2014).

9 Camus, *The Myth of Sisyphus and Other Essays*, 85.

10 Camus, *The Myth of Sisyphus and Other Essays*, 87–8.

11 See, for example, Roger Abrahams, *African American Folktales: Stories from Black Traditions in the New World* (New York: Pantheon Fairy Tale and Folklore Library, 1999).

Bibliography

1983 UAA Commission on Appraisal Report, *Empowerment: One Denomination's Quest for Racial Justice, 1967-1982*. Boston: Unitarian Universalist Association, 1993.

Abrahams, Roger D., *African American Folktales: Stories from Black Traditions in the New World*. New York: Pantheon Books, 1999.

Allen, Norm R., *African American Humanism: An Anthology*. Buffalo, NY: Prometheus, 1991.

—, *The Black Humanist Experience: An Alternative to Religion*. Buffalo, NY: Prometheus, 2002.

Altizer, Thomas J. J. and William Hamilton, *Radical Theology and the Death of God*. New York: The Bobbs-Merrill Company, Inc., 1966.

Anderson, Benedict, *Imagined Communities: Reflections on the Origin and Spread of Nationalism*. London and New York: Verso Books, 1983.

Anderson, Victor, *Beyond Ontological Blackness*. New York: Continuum, 1995.

Angell, Stephen and Anthony B. Pinn (eds), *Social Protest Thought in the African Methodist Episcopal Churchy, 1862-1939*. Knoxville: The University of Tennessee Press, 2000.

Baldwin, Lewis V., Rufus Burrow, Jr., Barbara A. Holmes, and Susan Holmes Winfield, *The Legacy of Martin Luther King, Jr.: The Boundaries of Law, Politics, and Religion*. Notre Dame, IN: University of Notre Dame Press, 2002.

Blum, Edward J., *W. E. B. Du Bois: American Prophet*. Philadelphia: University of Pennsylvania Press, 2007.

Bordo, Susan, "'Material Girl': The Effacements of Postmodern Culture," in Donn Welton (ed.), *Body and Flesh: A Philosophical Reader*. Malden, MA: Blackwell Publishers, Inc., 1998.

Brewer, J. Mason (ed.), *America's Negro Folklore*. Chicago: Quadrangle Books, 1968.

Bronner, Stephen Eric, *Camus: Portrait of a Moralist*. Chicago: University of Chicago Press, 2009.

Brown, Frank Burch, *Religious Aesthetics: A Theological Study of Making and Meaning*. Princeton: Princeton University Press, 2004.

Burrows, Rufus, *God and Human Dignity: The Personalism, Theology, and Ethics of Martin Luther King, Jr.* Notre Dame: University of Notre Dame Press, 2006.

Campbell, Colin, *Toward Sociology of Irreligion*. New York: Herder and Herder, 1972.

Camus, Albert, *The Myth of Sisyphus and Other Essays*. New York: Vintage International, 1991.

—, *Notebooks 1935-1942*. New York: Vintage International, 1991.

—, *The Rebel*. New York: Vintage International, 1991.

—, "The Renegade, or a Confused Mind," in trans. Carol Cosman, *Exile and the Kingdom*, New York: Vintage International, 2007.

Carrette, Jeremy R., *Foucault and Religion: Spiritual Corporality and Political Spirituality.* New York: Routledge, 2000.
Cone, James H., *A Black Theology of Liberation*, 20th Anniversary edn. Maryknoll, NY: Orbis Books, 1986.
—, *God of the Oppressed.* New York: Harper & Row, Publishers, 1975.
David, Grace, Pau Heelas, and Linda Woodhead (eds), *Predicting Religion: Christian, Secular and Alternative Futures.* Burlington, VT: Ashgate Publishing Company, 2003.
Dawkins, Richard, *The God Delusion*, rep. edn. New York: Mariner Books, 2008.
De Botton, Alain, *Religion for Atheists: A Non-Believer's Guide to the Uses of Religion.* New York: Vintage, 2013.
Dennett, Daniel, *Breaking the Spell: Religion as a Natural Phenomenon*, rep. edn. New York: Penguin Books, 2007.
Douglas, Kelly Brown, *The Black Christ.* Maryknoll, NY: Orbis Books, 1994.
—, *What's Faith Got to Do With It? Black Bodies/Christian Souls.* Maryknoll, NY: Orbis Books, 2005.
Douglass, Frederick, *Narrative of the Life of Frederick Douglass.* Boston: Anti-Slavery Office, 1845.
Du Bois, W. E. B., *Dusk of Dawn*, ed. Henry Louis Gates Jr., 1st edn. New York: Oxford University Press, 2014.
—, *The Souls of Black Folk.* New York: Vintage Books, 1990.
—, *The Souls of Black Folk.* Mineola, NY: Dover Publications, 1994.
Epstein, Greg, *Good Without God: What a Billion Nonreligious People Do Believe.* New York: William Morrow Paperbacks, 2010.
Forman, James, *The Making of Black Revolutionaries.* Washington, DC: Open Hand Publishing, 1985.
Foucault, Michel, *Ethics: Subjectivity and Truth*, ed. Paul Rabinow. New York: The New Press, 1997.
Girard, Rene, *Violence and the Sacred*, trans. Patrick Gregory. Baltimore: The Johns Hopkins University Press, 1977.
Goffman, Erving, *Stigma: Notes on the Management of Spoiled Identity.* New York: Simon & Schuster, 1963.
Grant, Jacquelyn, *White Women's Christ and Black Women's Jesus: Feminist Christology and Womanist Response.* Atlanta: Scholars Press, 1989.
Grayling, A. C., *Meditations for the Humanist: Ethics for a Secular Age.* New York: Oxford University Press, 2003.
—, *The God Argument: The Case Against Religion and for Humanism.* New York: Bloomsbury USA, 2013.
—, *The Good Book: A Humanist Bible*, rep. edn. London: Walker & Company, 2013.
Guralnick, Peter, *Searching for Robert Johnson: The Life and Legend of the "King of the Delta Blues Singers."* New York: Plume, 1998.
Hansberry, Lorraine, *A Raisin in the Sun.* With an introduction by Robert Nemiroff. New York: Vintage, 2004.
Harris, Sam, *The End of Faith: Religion, Terror, and the Future of Reason*, rep. edn. New York: W.W. Norton, 2005.
Harrison, Milmon F., *Righteous Riches: The Word of Faith Movement in Contemporary African American Religion.* New York: Oxford University Press, 2005.

Hitchens, Christopher, *God Is Not Great: How Religion Poisons Everything.* New York: Twelve, 2009.

Holly, James Theodore, "The Divine Plan of Human Redemption in Its Ethnological Development," in Anthony B. Pinn (ed.), *Moral Evil and Redemptive Suffering: A History of Theodicy in African-American Religious Thought.* Gainesville: University Press of Florida, 2002.

Hutchinson, Sikivu, *Godless Americana: Race and Religious Rebels.* Los Angeles: Infidel Books, 2013.

—, *Moral Combat: Black Atheists, Gender Politics, and the Values War.* Los Angeles: Infidel Books, 2011.

Jones, William R., *Is God a White Racist? A Preamble to Black Theology,* rev. edn. Boston: Beacon Press, 1998.

Kahn, Jonathon S., *Divine Discontent: The Religious Imagination of W. E. B. Du Bois.* New York: Oxford University Press, 2009.

Kass, Leon R., "What's Wrong With Babel?," in Georgy Wolfe (ed.), *The New Religious Humanists: A Reader.* New York: The Free Press, 1997.

Kellehear, Allan, *A Social History of Dying.* London: Cambridge University Press, 2007.

King, Martin L. Jr., "How Should a Christian View Communism?," in *Strength to Love.* Philadelphia: Fortress Press, 1963.

—, *Where Do We Go From Here: Chaos or Community?* Boston: Beacon Press, 1968.

Lackey, Michael, *African American Atheists and Political Liberation: A Study of the Sociocultural Dynamics of Faith.* Gainesville, FL: University Press of Florida, 2008.

Lee, Shayne, *T. D. Jakes: Americas New Preacher.* New York: New York University Press, 2005.

Lemert, Charles and Ann Branaman (eds), *The Goffman Reader.* Malden, MA: Blackwell Publishers, 1997.

Linden, David J., *The Compass of Pleasure: How Our Brains Make Fatty Foods, Orgasm, Exercise, Marijuana, Generosity, Vodka, Learning, and Gambling Feel So Good.* New York: Viking, 2011.

Margolick, David, *Strange Fruit: The Biography of a Song.* New York: Harper Perennial, 2001.

Marriott, Rob, "Last Testament," *Vibe Magazine.* November 1996.

Martin, Luther H., Huck Gutman, and Patrick H. Hutton (eds), *Technologies of the Self: A Seminar with Michel Foucault.* Amherst: The University of Massachusetts Press, 1988.

McHoul, Alec and Wendy Grace, *A Foucault Primer: Discourse, Power and the Subject.* New York: New York University Press, 1993.

Mellor, Philip A., "Death in High Modernity: The Contemporary Presence and Absence of Death," in David Clark (ed.), The *Sociology of Death.* Cambridge, MA: Blackwell Publishers, 1993, 11–30.

Morgan, David, *The Sacred Gaze: Religious Visual Culture in Theory and Practice.* Berkeley: University of California Press, 2005.

Morrison, Toni (ed.), *To Die for the People: The Writings of Huey P. Newton,* rep. edn. New York: Writers and Readers Publishing, Inc., 1995.

—, *Visual Piety: A History and Theory of Popular Religious Images.* Berkeley: University of California Press, 1998.

Moses, Wilson Jeremiah, *Black Messiahs and Uncle Toms: Social and Literary Manipulations of a Religious Myth.* University Park: The Pennsylvania State University Press, 1982.

—, *The Wings of Ethiopia: Studies in African-American Life and Letters*. Ames: Iowa University Press, 1990.
Patterson, Orlando, *Slavery and Social Death: A Comparative Study*. Cambridge: Harvard University Press, 1985.
Payne, Daniel, "Daniel Payne's Protestation of Slavery," in *Lutheran Herald and Journal of the Franckean Synod*. Fort Plain, NY: Committee of Publication of the Franckean Synod, 1839.
Pinn, Anthony B., *African American Humanist Principles: Living and Thinking Like the Children of Nimrod*. New York: Palgrave Macmillan, 2004.
—, *The Black Church in the Post-Civil Rights Era*. Maryknoll, NY: Orbis Books, 2002.
— (ed.), *By These Hands: A Documentary History of African American Humanism*. New York: New York University Press, 2001.
—, *Embodiment and the New Shape of Black Theological Thought*. New York: New York University Press, 2009.
—, *The End of God-Talk: An African American Humanist Theology*. Oxford: Oxford University Press, 2012.
— (ed.), *Moral Evil and Redemptive Suffering: A Documentary History*. Gainesville, FL: University Press of Florida, 2001.
—, *Moral Evil and Redemptive Suffering: A History of Theodicy in African-American Religious Thought*. Gainesville: University Press of Florida, 2002.
—, *Terror and Triumph: The Nature of Black Religion*. Minneapolis: Fortress Press, 2003.
— (ed.), *Theism and Public Policy: Humanist Responses*. New York: Palgrave Macmillan, 2014.
—, *Varieties of African American Religious Experience*. Minneapolis: Augsburg Fortress Press, 1998.
—, *Why, Lord? Suffering and Evil in Black Theology*. New York: Continuum, 1995.
—, "Atheists Gathering in Burbank: A Humanist Perspective," Religion Dispatches, October 27, 2009.
—, "Can Atheist Billboards Kill Religion?," Religion Dispatches, May 1, 2012.
— (guest ed.), "The Colors of Humanism," in a Special Issue of *Essays in the Philosophy of Humanism* 20 (2012): 23–30.
—, "God's Obituary: A Humanist Response to Mass Murder," Religion Dispatches, December 25, 2012.
—, "O(Pinn)ion: Reevaluating a Faith-Based Nation," Religion Dispatches, February 13, 2009.
—, "Thoughts on Martin Luther King, Jr.'s God, Humanist Sensibilities, and Moral Evil," *Theology Today* 65 (2008): 57–66.
—, "Thoughts on What Humanists Might Learn from Hip Hop," *Free Inquiry* 32 (2012): 31–5.
—, "Watch the Body With New Eyes: Womanist Thought's Contribution to a Humanist Notion of Ritual," *CrossCurrents* 57 (2007): 404–11.
Pinn, Anthony B. and Allen D. Callahan (eds), *African American Religious Life and the Story of Nimrod*. New York: Palgrave Macmillan, 2007.
Protero, Stephen, *American Jesus: How the Son of God Became a National Icon*. New York: Farrar, Straus and Giroux, 2003.
Shermer, Michael, *The Believing Brain: From Ghosts and Gods to Politics and Conspiracies – How We Construct Beliefs and Reinforce Them as Truths*. New York: Henry Holt, 2011.

Steinfels, Peter, "Scandinavian Nonbelievers, Which Is Not to Say Atheists," *New York Times*, February 27, 2009, http://www.nytimes.com/2009/02/28/us/28beliefs.html.
Sullivan, Nikki, *Tattooed Bodies: Subjectivity, Textuality, Ethics, and Pleasure*. Westport, CT: Praeger, 2001.
Thoreau, Henry David, *Walden*. Princeton: Princeton University Press, 1970.
Washington, James (ed.), *A Testament of Hope: The Essential Writings of Martin Luther King, Jr.* New York: HarperCollins, 1986.
Welch, Sharon, *A Feminist Ethic of Risk*. Minneapolis: Fortress Press, 2000.
West, Cornel, *Prophesy Deliverance! An Afro-American Revolutionary Christianity*. Philadelphia: Westminster John Knox, 1982.
Williams, Delores, *Sisters in the Wilderness*. Maryknoll, NY: Orbis Books, 1993.
Wilmore, Gayraud, *Black Religion and Black Radicalism: An Interpretation of the Religious History of Afro-American People*, 2nd edn. Maryknoll, NY: Orbis Books, 1983. First Published 1972 by Doubleday.
Wright, Richard, *Black Boy*. New York: Harper & Row Publishers, 1966.
—, *Black Boy*. New York: Harper Perennial Modern Classics, 2007.
—, *The Outsider*. Library of America Edition. New York: HareperPerennial, 1991.
—, "The Man Who Lived Underground," *In Eight Men: stories*. New York: HarperPerennial, 1996.
Yancy, George (ed.), *Christology and Whiteness*. New York: Routledge, 2012.

Discography (Sound recordings)

"Buked and Scorned." Negrospirituals.com. Accessed March 21, 2011. http://www.negrospirituals.com/news-song/buked_and_scorned.htm.
"Nobody Knows De Trouble I've Had." Negrospirituals.com. Accessed March 21, 2011. http://www.negrospirituals.com/news-song/nobody_knows_de_trouble_i.htm.
"Ride on King Jesus." Negrospirituals.com. Accessed March 21, 2011. http://www.negrospirituals.com/news-song/ride_on_king_jesus.htm.
"There Is a Balm in Gilead." Negrospirituals.com. Accessed March 21, 2011. http://www.negrospirituals.com/news-song/there_is_a_blam_in_gilead.htm.
Carter, Shawn (Jay Z), "Moment of Clarity," *The Black Album*. © 2003 by Roc-A-Fella/Def Jam. New York. Compact Disc.
—, *Magna Carta*. © 2013 by Roc-A-Fella Records. New York. Compact Disc.
Carter, Shawn (Jay Z) and Kanye West, *Watch the Throne*. © 2011 by Roc-A-Fella Records. New York. Compact Disc.
Shakur, Tupac, "All Eyez on Me," *All Eyez on Me*. © 1996 by Death Row/Interscope Records. Los Angeles. Compact Disc.
—, "Only God Can Judge Me," *All Eyez on Me*. © 1996 by Death Row/Interscope Records. Los Angeles. Compact Disc.
—, *The Don Killuminati: The 7 Day Theory*. © 1996 by Death Row Records. Los Angeles. Compact Disc.
—, "Blasphemy," *The Don Killuminati: The 7 Day Theory*. © 1996 by Death Row Records. Los Angeles. Compact Disc.
—, "Hail Mary," *The Don Killuminati: The 7 Day Theory*. © 1996 by Death Row Records. Los Angeles. Compact Disc.

Index

absurdism
   absurd heroes   59
   hip-hop and absurdity   121, 130, 133, 135
   and nontheism   24
   relation to humanism   147
   theistic faith as absurd   117
   world as absurd   1, 5, 80, 148
African American Humanism   2, 7, 24–5, 59
   strategies for growth of   27
African Americans for Humanism (AAH)   26
anti-racism   7
atheology   107

Baker, Ella   18
Black Jesus   84–8, 130–2
blackness   8, 76, 77
   as moral problem   49
Black Realism   24

Calvinism   77
Camus, Albert   59, 97, 113, 127, 130, 153, 164–6
challenge of three   1, 5–7, 153
Christology   8, 17, 73, 75, 79–80, 82, 83
   as model of human self-understanding   77
   problems with   86–92
color line   44, 50
Cone, James   44, 73, 84, 136

death of God theology   74
Douglas, Kelly Brown   73, 83, 86
Du Bois, W. E. B   40–54, 128, 149
   double consciousness   50

Ethical Culture   4, 69, 97–8, 100–3

functional ultimacy   13
fundamentalism   38, 117–18, 145

God
   as restraint   61–6, 69
Grant, Jacquelyn   85
Great Migration   17

Harlem Renaissance   21, 24, 134
hip-hop   8–9, 23, 84–5, 113, 118–22, 124–6, 127, 129–31, 133, 135, 151
Houston Oasis   104–7, 109
humanism
   and blues   19–20
   naturalistic   19–22
   principles of   3
   shadowed   15–19
   and theology   62
Hurston, Zora Neale   25

irreligion   97, 109

Jones, William R.   6, 13, 115

King, Martin Luther
   and Personalism   18, 69
   theological beliefs   8, 141

liberal religion   7, 15, 23, 83, 100
liberation theology   43, 44, 49, 73, 91, 136

Martin, Trayvon   29–32, 39, 40
millennials   99, 103
modus agendi   59, 61, 62

INDEX

nihilism 1, 121, 147–9
Nimrod 57–68
Nones 5, 26, 99

ordinary
   ritualization of 100, 102, 110–12

performative diversity 122
pragmatism 42, 45
prosperity gospel 18, 37, 118, 123

racism 11–15, 23, 29–32, 40, 43, 45, 46, 76, 84, 86, 88, 116, 125, 136, 137
Rauschenbusch, Walter 141
religious naturalism 42, 45, 53
Roberts, J. Deotis 84

secularization 99
Shakur, Tupac 84, 130–1
Sisyphus 1–2, 8–9, 58–9, 147–51
slavery 30–1, 33, 35, 36, 81, 86, 128
Social Gospel 15, 18, 43, 44, 141

somebodyness 69–71
spirituals 16, 19, 51, 54, 79–80, 128, 135
suffering 46, 47, 51–2, 66, 68, 71–4
   normalization of 86–90
suicide 1
Sunday Assembly 8, 102–4

theism
   distinction with religion 94–7
theodicy 46, 68, 74
Thug Life 130–2
tragic soul-life 50–2
Turner, Henry McNeal 17, 83

Unitarian Universalist Association (UUA) 21, 97–8, 100–3

Walker, Alice 25
whiteness 8, 76–7
   in contrast to blackness
     in theology 81–92
Wright, Richard 21, 24, 134, 149

www.ingramcontent.com/pod-product-compliance
Lightning Source LLC
Chambersburg PA
CBHW050140240426
43673CB00043B/1740